Making It!

Case studies of successful Canadian visual artists.

Making It!

Case studies of successful Canadian visual artists.

CHRISTOPHER TYRELL

C.T. PRODUCTIONS
VANCOUVER, CANADA
2011

Published by C.T. Productions
c/o London Place
1177 Hornby Street, #707
Vancouver, British Columbia, Canada
V6Z 2E9
www.christyrell.ca

LIBRARY AND ARCHIVES CANADA CATALOGUING IN PUBLICATION

Tyrell, Chris, 1947-
Making it : case studies of successful Canadian visual artists /
by Chris Tyrell

Includes index.

ISBN 978-0-9809528-1-0

1. Art—economic aspects—Canada. 2. Art—Canada. 3. Artists—Canada.
I. Title.

N6545.6.T98 2011 706.8'8 C2010-907662-1

Transcription: Jessica Nitowski
Editing by: Beth Kaplan
Cover and Design by: Chris Tyrell
Printing: Ray Hignell Services Inc., Winnipeg. Manitoba, Canada

Thank you!

I am extremely grateful to all the artists whose words are recorded in this book. Their willingness to share their professional experiences for the benefit of upcoming generations of Canadian visual artists is wondrous creative and intellectual philanthropy.

I am very grateful for the assistance of Scott Cronshaw of Opus Framing and Art Supplies, Nancy Wise of Sandhill Book Marketing, editor Beth Kaplan, transcriber Jessica Nitowski, and friends Dwight Koss and Stephen Schilling without whose help this book would not have been undertaken.

I am also very grateful to Sadira Rodrigues, Amy Clausen, Terry Plummer, Valerie Ceppi, John Skibinski, and the wonderful and patient technicians who support the Continuing Studies Department at Emily Carr University. I am very grateful for the opportunities and support that they have given me. I am also greatly indebted to my students whose questions, passion and spirit so inspire me.

Chris Tyrell
Vancouver, 2011

Index

Caveats

This primer is B.C.- and Vancouver-centric. I set out to provide information to serve all Canadian artists, but I am proud to place an emphasis on artists from my community to illustrate the business principles I celebrate here. Google and other search engines make it easy for artists anywhere in the country to identify resources in your area and online.

I, Christopher Tyrell, cannot be held liable for any and all advice offered in this book or for any outcomes resulting from the application of advice provided herein. This book is a compendium of advice designed to be of assistance and not to replace the professional involvement of accountants, lawyers and marketers in your career development.

Preface

My first book, *Artist Survival Skills: How to Make a Living as a Canadian Visual Artist* (2008), documented some business standards for Canadian visual artists.

In this book, I set out to celebrate some business practices that have significantly contributed to the development of a visual artist's career. Each chapter may be about the entirety of a career or it may be about one aspect of a career. It is my hope that in these stories, you will find inspiration or a comfortable methodology to apply to your own practice.

These are not "how-to" stories, although some chapters provide specific directions. Rather, they are narratives intended to inspire and provoke you. These stories prove that the routes to success are many and varied. Each chapter is an interview with one or more artists:

1. CHAPTER ONE: Because face-to-face sales is the preferred experience of art buyers and earn artists (almost) full retail value, this chapter is a panel discussion with **Rachael Ashe, Leanne Christie, Sonja Hebert, Mary Ann Tateishi** and **Richard Tetrault** about their experiences with inter-personal sales.
2. CHAPTER TWO: I interviewed **Shawn O'Hagan** because she has excelled with Internet sales through Etsy.com. But what is really remarkable about her, is her capacity to adapt. Her creative products changed dramatically when she relocated to an isolated small town.

3. Chapter Three: Because mailing list management and effective commercial communication are vital skills you must have, this chapter is an interview with **Rachael Ashe** and **Kristine Paton** about *Mail Chimp* and *Constant Contact*—two incredibly practical websites.
4. Chapter Four: **Leslie Redhead** also makes effective use of the Internet in her practice. Her blog is a perfect professional model.
5. Chapter Five: **Jude Griebel**'s success with artist residencies has provided him with a rich source of inspiration and professional development. His story provides an excellent model for the emerging artist intent on a life-long professional career and for mid-career artists needing rejuvenation.
6. Chapter Six: **Madeleine Wood** faced a decision a great many mid-career artists consider: Should I quit my job and support myself exclusively by my creative practice?
7. Chapter Seven: By developing a vibrant sideline artistic career while he is employed full-time, **Gary Sim** will be able to retire into an established dynamic career.
8. Chapter Eight: **Davyd Oram** is a young and enterprising artist who has discovered unique ways to underwrite his practice and teaching materials.
9. Chapter Nine: **Joyce Kamikura** has an interesting story to tell about licensing her work for reproduction. It earned her considerable income, but the experience was not what she expected so she has valuable advice to share.
10. Chapter Ten: **Lee Bacchus** found a way to advance sales of his work. His is an important story because many artists, for different reasons, find sales and self-advocacy to be a significant challenge.
11. Chapter Eleven: **Ross Penhall** changed media to his great financial and creative advantage. Not only that, he did so painting in the highly competitive genre of landscape painting.

12. Chapter Twelve: **Marina Bychkova** is a master of niche marketing. Her uplifting story is about a childhood passion that becomes an income-earning juggernaut.
13. Chapter Thirteen: **Richard Tetrault**'s approach to community and public art has greatly benefited both Vancouver's Downtown Eastside and his career.
14. Chapter Fourteen: **Tiko Kerr** dramatically earned the critical respect he wanted by turning adversity into triumph.
15. Chapter Fifteen: Because I am asked about representation more than any other topic, this chapter is a panel discussion with **Kitty Blandy, Marcus Bowcott, Tiko Kerr**, and **Val Mason** about their experiences with commercial art galleries.

If you are a contemporary artist creating "speculative" work, you are involved in a relatively new profession.

In the mid-90s, geological analyses of Indian cave petroglyphs dated the paintings found on quartzite cave walls to 290,000 years before the dawn of the Christian era. But it was not until 1863, when Napoleon III granted the 3000 artists rejected from the Salon de Paris the right to show their work in an annex to the official exhibition, that the "l'art pour l'art" ("art for art's sake") movement began. The new movement encouraged artists to take risks and emphasized the creation of "speculative" work over commissioned work. *Artists have only been selling self-inspired work for less than 150 years!*

Artists are society's heart, soul and voice yet a great many artists struggle to survive off their creative practice. The collective experience of the generous artists whose stories are told in this book add up to centuries of experience that inform and inspire.

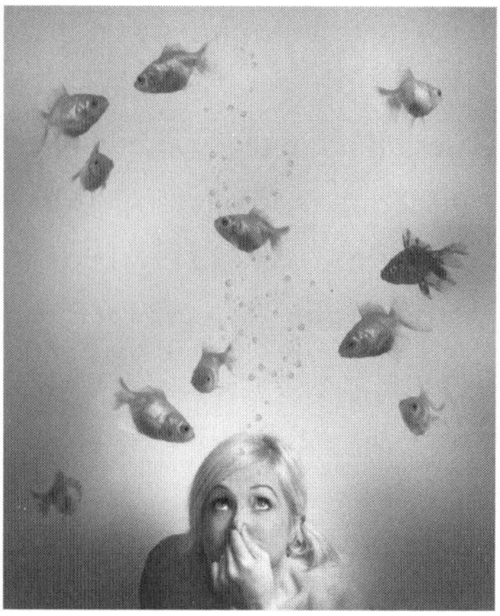

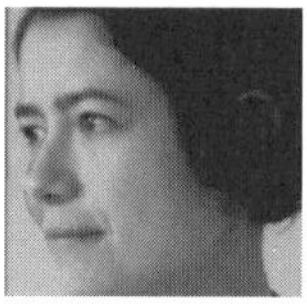

RACHAEL ASHE, 1972
Underneath an imaginary sea; photography
2009; 9.5" x 11.5"

http://rachaelashe.com

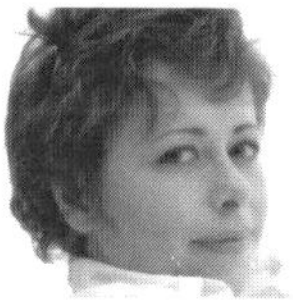

LEANNE CHRISTIE, 1974
A Sabrina Sunday; oil on canvas
2010; 24" x 24"

www.leanne-christie.com

1 Face-to-Face Sales

Rachael Ashe, Leanne Christie, Sonja Hébert, Mary Anne Tateishi and Richard Tetrault talk about inter-personal sales.

Date of interview: October 6, 2010

"Artists who do well with face-to-face sales are those who are willing to engage with people. It's the artists who sit quietly and think that their art is going to sell itself who go home hungry."

— *Leanne Christie*

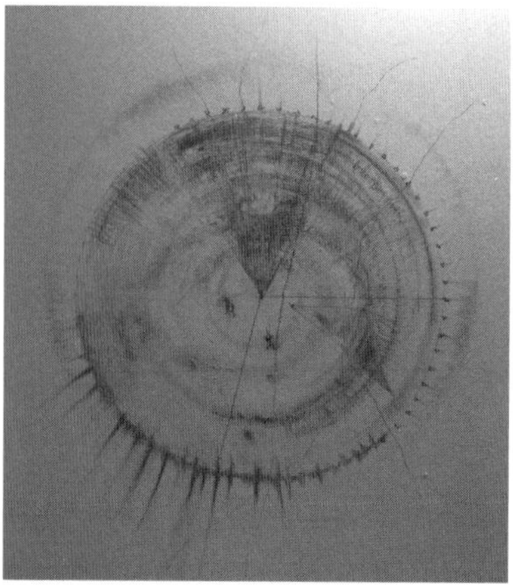

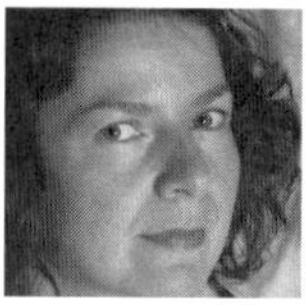

SONJA HÉBERT, 1968

Sillage (detail); graphite directly on gallery wall
2009; 30" x 30" (as an element within an installation)

www.sonjaportfolio.ca

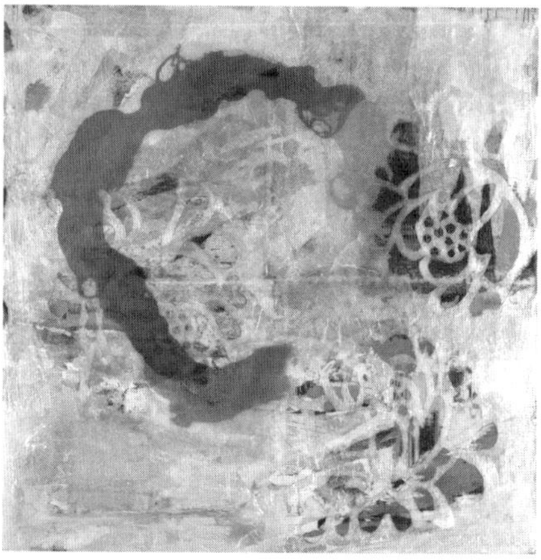

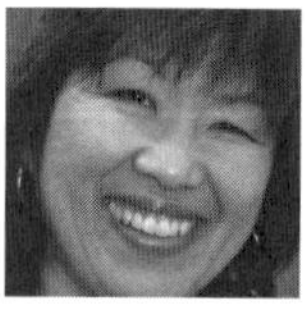

MARY ANNE TATEISHI

Wreath; mixed media on panel with resin
2010; 40" x 40"

www.matart.ca

PROLOGUE

In 2008, the online community of artists, Myartclub.com, conducted a consumer survey to gain insight into the market in which their member artists were selling work. That survey quantified consumer attitudes of art buyers, and what stood out was the strength of consumer demand for direct contact with artists. Art consumers indicated a very strong desire for the "back story" of their purchases and/or of the artist, and they wanted to hear it directly from the artist. When you understand visual art customer preferences, you realize the importance of face-to-face sales.

Artists consistently report that an astonishingly high percentage of their sales are to people with whom they have a relationship. Although the term "relationship" is undefined, the importance of the statement to artists cannot be overestimated. Regardless of the nature of your relationships—relative, friend, neighbour, acquaintance or colleague—you should strive to create as many relationships as possible throughout your career, and conduct as many of your sales as possible in person.

You can make and grow your relationships in many ways. At the base of the relationship/sales pyramid for everyone, however, is a mailing list. There is nothing more important for an artist than a comprehensive mailing list, if you want to have a successful and reasonably lucrative creative practice. Once you have a list, communicating regularly (but not too often) to its members with compelling communications becomes your ideal communications strategy.

The past decade has seen incredible technological advancements in networking websites, software and hardware that have changed the way relationships are managed. These web-based tools make direct personal sales increasingly important to the careers of artists, especially since direct sales earn the full retail price for the work. Regardless of these technological developments, however, face-to-face contact remains critically important for the development of relationships with the people on your mailing list. If you meet your customers in person, the relationships become significant.

There are many ways to meet your customers. The obvious ones are at exhibitions, studio visits and sales, but these types of get-togethers are often busy public events that prevent you from spending quality time with anyone. Instead, these types of events are effective for establishing quick per-

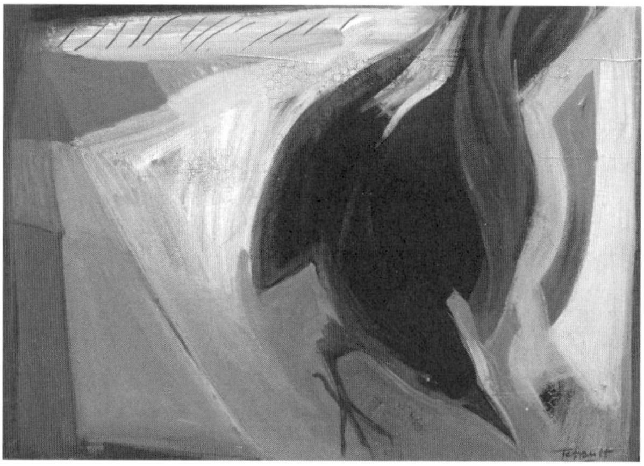

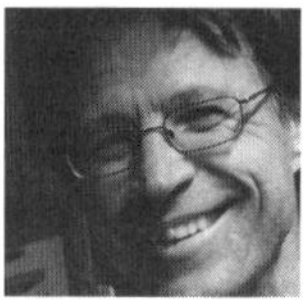

RICHARD TETRAULT, 1951
Crow From Above; acrylic on board
2010; 24" x 30"

http://richard-tetrault.ca

sonal contact with as many people as possible so that a deeper connection can be made later. Getting contact information at crowded events is as important as making sales.

Customers prefer educational interaction with artists, so studio sales that include a demonstration (or in some other way provides a glimpse into your creative process) is ideal. The contacts you make at busy events will become meaningful if you follow-up after the event quickly with an email that expands on the education; to be powerful, the follow-up communications should avoid the subject of sales and include interesting information.

In most cities, the studio sales of artists are very popular with both the artists and the public. Artist-organized events that bring the public into the artists' studios (such as Vancouver's Artists in Our Midst, Eastside Culture Crawl, The Drift, etcetera) are now well established and highly attended community festivals. They provide vital face-to-face opportunities for you to advance your relationships with established clientele and to meet vast numbers of potential new customers.

These area-specific open studio events involve a lot of preparatory work; many artists who participate in them, use them as a deadline. If you are an artist who has participated in an event like The Crawl and has complained about the amount of work involved, think of what it is like to operate a booth all year round, as Leanne Christie does.

To gain insight into direct personal sales, I invited several artists to discuss their experiences. On October 6th, they joined me in the offices of Vancouver's Alliance for Arts and Culture to talk. The assembled artists were:

1. **Rachael Ashe.**
Rachael Ashe is a Vancouver-based artist working in photography, mixed media collage, and altered book arts. She is motivated by a need to experiment with different styles and techniques; much of her work is inspired by nature and imagination. Her work has been shown in Toronto, Vancouver, Salt Lake City, Los Angeles, San Francisco, Portland and the UK and published in numerous books and magazines.

2. **Leanne Christie**

Leanne Christie is a South African-born oil painter now residing in Vancouver. Upon completion of her degree at Rhodes University, she embarked on ten years of exploration in Europe, spending a large portion of her time based in London, U.K. In her years abroad, Leanne dedicated herself to understanding her desire to paint and its value as a medium in the contemporary world. For many years, she separated herself from the moniker of artist, preferring that of painter. Leanne's subject is the medium itself, with her choice of imagery simply serving the role of translator between viewer and artist.

3. **Sonja Hébert**.

Sonja Hébert has been living and creating in Vancouver for 19 years. Since receiving her degree from the Emily Carr University of Art + Design, she has continued to develop her practice through international and national art residencies, local art events and self-directed projects. Her works have been exhibited in British Columbia and other parts of Canada. The main themes in her work are of dislocation, hybridization, the cycles of life and adaptation. Sonja's drawings are made of charcoal, graphite, oil sticks and découpage. Her choices of media for installation are varied and include unconventional sculptural materials and altered objects.

4. **Mary Anne Tateishi**.

Mary Anne Tateishi came to painting after careers in advertising, retail and motherhood. She paints on wood panel, using tissue, acrylic paints, and resin. Her painting process uses layering, transparency and vivid colour to explore ideas of time and memory. Her work is in private and public collections across Canada, as well as in the U.S.A., Europe, and Japan. She has been interviewed on CBC Radio, City TV and Fairchild Television, and her work has appeared in local newspapers and arts magazines.

5. **Richard Tetrault**

Richard Tetrault is a Canadian born painter, printmaker, muralist and educator based in Vancouver. Working out of a studio in East Vancouver, he explores the shifting dynamics of the urban landscape in various media. As a muralist, he has painted numerous works in Mexico, Argentina, the United States and Canada. He has also coordinated a range of collaborative, publicly situated murals throughout Vancouver. Recently, working with urban Aboriginal artists, he coordinated a 7600 square foot mural—the largest mural in Western Canada. *Painted Lives and Shifting Landscapes* (Anvil Press, 2004) documents his work over the past thirty years.

Links to the websites and venues mentioned by the artists during the conversation are provided in the chapter epilogue.

INTERVIEW

Chris: Could we start with introductions, please?

Sonja: I have been a professional artist since 2002, and my practice encompasses drawing and installation work. I am involved with face-to-face sales, but much of my practice involves creating non-commercial work. My experience with the sales of my drawings has been through studio visits and events such as the Main Street Art Drift, Eastside Culture Crawl, and Cheaper Show #9.

Leanne: I moved to Canada from the U.K. two years ago. I'm an oil painter and I consider myself to be professional. My two years in Vancouver have been a baptism of fire in terms of face-to-face sales; my booth in the Granville Island Public Market is pretty much a permanent thing that has supported me for the past two years.

I sell 8" by 10" canvases and recently started selling 24" square work that has been selling fairly well. I also sell miniatures that are collectibles; I like having some work that is simple and well priced on my table. I only sell originals; I don't make prints. I am, however, playing around with an idea about a children's colouring book—again, to have something that's easy to put on the table that doesn't require a huge amount of effort. I want to focus on painting.

Mary Anne: I'm a painter. I do large mixed media, layered works. I've been painting for about ten years. Before that, I had careers in retail, advertising and marketing. I've been in the Culture Crawl since 2005; I was also in Cheaper Show #9 this year, and I did the Toronto Outdoor Art Exhibition last year. I'm also in several galleries, and I hold open studios as well.

Rachael: I am a photographer, and I alter books; in the past, I've also made jewellery. I'm originally from Toronto and have more experience with sales there. I've been using the Internet as a medium to sell my work and build exposure since coming to Vancouver six and a half years ago. I've been using Flickr, my blog, and Twitter to let people know about the new work that I've created, and using Etsy as an online venue to sell work.

Richard: I'm a painter, printmaker, muralist, and my studio work covers a broad range of mediums and processes, ranging from acrylics, woodcuts, linocuts and monotypes to mixed media works on various surfaces. My focus, over more than thirty years, has been on developing series that reflect the dynamics of the city. I don't work to any specific market, but rather follow my own instincts, concerns and directions. Overall, co-operatives and studio collectives have been an important part of my art experience.

Perhaps a good place to start for me is with the Eastside Culture Crawl. In the mid 90s, a bunch of us that had been doing different things at different times thought it would be an idea to fuse the dates of our open studios. We collaborated and ended up deciding on a strategic weekend just prior to Christmas. In the beginning, it was just artists in 1000 Parker Street plus the building I am in here in Strathcona, Paneficio Studios. There were maybe 20 of us involved then, and now there are over 300 artists opening their studios and lots and lots of buildings. We're a non-profit organization now; we do community outreach with school kids, there's preview shows, and we do exhibitions at the PNE (Pacific National Exhibition) each summer. And all of what we do is built on the success of the Crawl.

Tens of thousands of people attend, and for me, it's a reason to organize my studio. You have to get organized for the Crawl. My partner, Esther, is a photographer, and we take the Crawl seriously. If the work is considered, well thought out and well presented, viewers will respond. We want to make an impact with our display so that sales happen—they don't always happen immediately, but they do happen, and I think it's because we put together a really good exhibit each year. We don't show the same thing twice, and we make it interesting for people to hang out in our space. Artists who succeed with the Crawl treat it as a professional venue, taking time to self-curate to make it work.

The Crawl provides you with a great opportunity to distribute information. I do a lot of networking around mural projects and see people I haven't seen for ages. It's about networking as much as anything.

Chris: You're saying that the Crawl is more than an event, that it's a community. It sounds like an artist-run centre with no building.

Richard: Exactly. We talk every year about having a physical space, but there are overhead and other implications, so thus far, the artists' studios provide the spaces and the Crawl is a network that unites us. The Crawl is organization, hype, media and critical mass. Artists pay to be members; we currently have more than 300 members, and we receive a fair number of grants. We earn about a third of our annual revenue from the advertising in our brochure each year.

Chris: What advice would you give to students about face-to-face sales?

Rachael: That it's important to do your research and to develop a proper system for pricing your work. So many artists don't price their work properly. Whether you use a price-per-square-inch method or one based on hours, you have to have a system—and don't be afraid to ask people for feedback about your prices. Another thing is to track how much time you spend on your work. I think a lot of artists fail to do that.

Sonja: Although my practice is less focused on sales, I've made representation and being active within communities my priorities. But when I have been more sales-focused, I've found that the best venue was my studio. I create events in my studio that teach visitors something.

If I am going on a residency, for example, I find that people like learning about what I'm going to be creating. Or if I'm doing a special project, people want to know about it, so I create an art talk to explain it. I show drawings of my work, and I answer questions, and I let people know why I need money. I explain why I am having the show and sale, and I find it works marvelously for sales. People have been extremely supportive. Sometimes people like a piece but may not really want to buy anything, but knowing that I need money for a trip or a project makes the sale happen.

When I've had to fundraised for myself, and I've always been able to earn the money that I needed. I think you need to be very clear and honest with people—tell them what you do and why you want to do it. Show them your work, and tell them why you're creating it. Being open and honest about your intentions creates really a good rapport with people. I've maintained good relationships with people who want to know how my career is going. Consequently, when my studio burnt down recently, my community came forth and said, "Hey, we're going to help you out."

Chris: You're saying that "purpose" provides a good incentive to buy. That's a great strategy.

Sonja: It's helped me a lot. I might need money to create an installation that will be ephemeral, but I will show them drawings of it that I can sell in order to keep creating. Sometimes the drawing is about the proposed work, but sometimes it's about another topic altogether.

Mary Anne: So how did you develop your relationship with these dedicated people?

Sonja: I meet a lot of people in various contexts, sometimes artistic and sometimes not. I value each connection and keep in touch whenever possible. I use email, and I still phone people—some people prefer the phone—and I've even written postcards or notes to keep in touch. I always keep in mind that I have these relationships, and I enjoy the rapport I have with people. I guess I see it as part of belonging to a place or a community. I reach out to people who have shown an interest in my work or me, and I keep them up to date with what's happening in my career.

I don't know if sales are related to a mindset or not, but when I participated in Cheaper Show #9—and Mary Anne, you were there too, so I'm curious about your experience—I assumed everybody would sell. I mean, everything at the Cheaper Show sells for $200, so I was surprised when artists said to me, “Congratulations! You sold your art!”

My sales there represented a financial loss! Each of my pieces in the show was worth a thousand dollars, but I sold each of them for two hundred—the price hardly paid for the materials! But I participated in it because it was an opportunity to build community and to support the initiative of other artists. And it draws a lot of people. I think it's important to be in some high profile events in order to achieve a certain level of local recognition. I was clear, going into it, that it was about potential opportunity and not about making money from a sale.

Chris: So by participating in the Cheaper Show, you're underselling your work enormously?

Sonja: I put my best pieces forward, and all the other artists who did the same were definitely underselling. But for artists, this is not an event about selling in the way that it is for the attending public. This is supposed to be about creating opportunities for people—for artists to make new business relations, and for folks who are new to art to be able to afford something they’re excited about and that normally might not be within their means.

Mary Anne: There is a tremendous amount of hype around the Cheaper Show. You believe that if you get in the show, you've really accomplished something! I found out I was in it by watching the announcement broadcast on the Web at six in the morning. There was a big build-up on how many applications they had received and how selective they'd had to be, and then they announced the winners and started flashing artist’s names, one by one. I was sitting there, and when I saw my name, I said, "Oh my God, I'm in!" And I ran upstairs and woke up my husband with "I'm in the Cheaper Show!

Chris: Given what you earn in this venue, why is this exciting?

Mary Anne: Because they have a curator's night, and they invite special buyers. They do things to promote you; they call the show a career-launcher. On the preview night, the room was packed with lots of important people from the art community.

Sonja: The preview night was by invitation only. What disappointed me was that the works were numbered, and the numbers were supposed to be covered up that night to make sure that the attendees didn't have an advantage the next day when the works went on sale. But they didn't cover the numbers, so on opening night, people who knew what number work they wanted could go directly to the cashier to buy it.

My work sold within five minutes. Nobody was in yet, but all of a sudden a "sold" sticker was on one of my pieces and then soon thereafter, the other. I had written a letter that I put on the back of each piece, thinking that the buyer would be somebody that normally didn't buy art, but I think it went to a gallerist or a collector who could sell it for what it was worth. In some ways, I felt really ripped off by the experience.

Mary Anne: My work went right away too, and I wasn't even in the room. It's a value issue. The organizers encourage you to put a highly-valued piece in the show, even though they're all going to sell for one low price—all to ensure a big audience for the show

I think in some ways there is a lack of feedback for artists in Vancouver. I don't get the sense that curators here visit artist studios very often. Gallery owners say they're getting so many submissions that they don't need to do studio visits anymore. They can just look at websites. I was in Winnipeg recently and noticed that curators were scheduling studio visits all the time. If we had more of that in Vancouver, I think people wouldn't have to take a loss to get noticed.

Richard: Gallery owners still come out. I don't know much about the Cheaper Show, but there are many other ways where you can show work that doesn't require that you give it away for a hundred dollars. When I show in The Crawl, I sell at the same price as I do in a commercial gallery, but at The Crawl, I get full retail when I sell.

You can't vary your prices, or you'll never sell. People will wait for your work until it comes up at a discounted event. Charity auctions, however, are a different thing. At an auction, I'll put a reserve price on my work. Otherwise, I don't think that fluctuating prices is a good idea. It undermines the value of your work.

I know what you're saying about the lack of venues, Mary Anne, and I think that's a serious issue in Vancouver. In East Vancouver, there are a few good venues where you can show commercially to a large audience—The Cultch (Vancouver East Cultural Centre), Britannia Library and a few small galleries on Commercial Drive—but there's not much else.

Sonja: I think it's important to stay current with certain people who are not necessarily interested in sales; it's about having another kind of currency. I realize now that I'm not going to find those people through events like the Cheaper Show. I thought I might.

Richard: I like what you were saying about your "Cristo-style" approach to raising funds for a project, Sonja. Installations can take years to realize; funding them by selling your work and not by corporate sponsorship is a really interesting approach.

Chris: *An advantage of The Crawl is that it involves seeing the artists in their studios. You get rich contextual information when you visit artists in the comfort of their own studios. Plus, paying directly to the artist can be as fulfilling for the buyer as for the seller.*

Mary Anne: I think the organizers did a great job of attracting people to the Cheaper Show that would never go to a studio or a gallery. There were lots of people in their twenties. It was like a party, and I think that people get inspired about art from these kinds of events.

Richard: Both events (The Crawl and Cheaper Show) are festivals, they're events that bring people out. They encourage people to get involved with art in a way that is not intimidating. I just wonder about that hundred dollar price; I mean, that is giving your art away. What are you getting back for it?

Mary Anne: I think maybe you do the Cheaper Show once. Sonja impressed me because she was hanging around her painting and talking to people about her work. I thought that was smart. I couldn't do that because mine was in the corner.

Chris: What about you, Leanne?

Leanne: My experience with face-to-face sales is very much nuts and bolts because that's how I keep a roof over my head. Selling my artwork is my only source of income. If I were speaking to somebody just starting out, I would tell them that their success or failure in face-to-face sales doesn't reflect on the quality of their artwork.

I've seen quite a few artists whose work is mediocre do extremely well, and I've also seen artists who do truly superb work really struggle. Artists who do well with face-to-face sales are those who are willing to engage with people. It's the artists who sit quietly and think that their art is going to sell itself, who go home hungry.

Although I will get a few discerning buyers who see my work and say, "This is something I want," there's not enough of those people around to make my living. An emerging artist like me, with incredibly reasonable prices, can't be relying on that one person who identifies with my work. I have to take the initiative to make enough sales happen.

Although face-to-face selling is the most rewarding thing I've ever done, it can also be brutal. You need to have a certain type of personality in order to survive it. You need to be professional, full stop; you need to go into the studio every day, and you need to have stamina.

The work is exhausting. I am forever setting things up, taking them down, looking for opportunities, filling out applications and keeping up with my clients. I'm constantly making follow-up calls and trying to figure out how to market myself. And you have to keep your energy up, even when you're feeling sick or tired or you're feeling low. You have to have the energy to say, "Hey, how are you doing?" to a complete stranger. Then, while they're trying to figure out if you want to sell them something, you have to try to make that connection.

It takes a thick skin to keep it up. The rejection that you can experience in face-to-face sales can be awful, but the worst type of rejection is when you become invisible—when nobody sees you. Days like those are the counter-balance to those fantastic glory days when suddenly everybody wants to talk to you and buy your work. You have to be able to keep a level head and balance the highs and the lows.

You need to know who you are and why you're there—especially when you're standing next to another vendor who's got security guards to carry their bags to their Ferraris because they've had such a great day and you haven't made a sale in three days. I know that I'm there to earn enough money to continue to paint. Painting is my passion, and that's why I am there selling every day. I don't do it to become rich; I'm selling in order to be able to be in the studio investigating what I can do with paint.

The best thing about face-to-face sales is that you get to be involved in your client's lives. You meet so many people. Being a painter can be a solitary experience, but when you talk with clients, they tell you stories about your art, about the joy it's bought to them; it is really rewarding. So yeah, face-to-face sales are not for everybody. How you do has a lot to do with how you interact with people.

Chris: How many days per week are you on Granville Island?

Leanne: It varies. On average I'm there two weeks out of every month. That way, I know there'll be decent income coming in. And I do a lot of commissions on a very casual basis—there's no deposits or anything. I do a couple of pieces for people who want me to do something, and they can come and choose one. If there's nothing that connects with them, they can walk away free, but they've had a fantastic experience. They've gained understanding about the painting process, and we've had a fantastic experience together.

Chris: And you get these commissions from exposure on Granville Island?

Leanne: I was in a gallery when I first arrived in Vancouver, but after a year they told me I needed to make a decision, because selling on Granville Island was not compatible with their image. I chose to stay with the Island.

People may look down on the way I sell on the Island, but I meet so many people—everybody in Vancouver seems to walk through it. It's like a meeting square in the old towns, where you'll have both the king and the pauper walk past you. You meet people from every walk of life.

Chris: Do you have a sense of what percentage of your customers are local people and what percentage are tourists?

Leanne: I would say probably 90% are local.

Chris: What would you tell emerging artists about face-to-face sales, Mary Anne?

Mary Anne: I think your relationship with the buyer is the key issue. Everything you do has to build your relationships. When you're selling, you have to have your business cards out and a place for people to sign up to be on your mailing list. As Richard said, lots of times people come in when you're really busy and can't talk. You need to give them a way to contact you. Sometimes they'll call you later. Lots of things can happen after the event is over.

You can't set goals like, "I made X number of dollars at The Crawl last year, and this year I want to make more." There are too many factors you can't control—the weather could be bad, there could be lots of competition—all you can control are goals such as, "Okay, I'm going to make sure I get 20 new people for my mailing list." Or "I'm going to make sure I really connect with a few people and then follow up."

I would tell emerging artists to get a studio. And if you can, find a mentor, a person with face-to-face sales experience. When I first got into my studio, I was sharing with another artist who had been in the building for at least five years before me. She gave me a lot of valuable professional tips.

I offer to take several paintings to a client's house, so that they can try them out if they're not sure about a painting. Once you get into somebody's home, you can offer useful suggestions on how the art can work in their space. And on my website, I have photographs of my paintings in peoples' homes. I think it gives potential clients confidence in my work, plus the idea that my art looks great in a home. It also shows that I have relationships with my buyers.

You have to be comfortable talking to people. You can't be sullen or have an attitude. One thing great about the Crawl is what can happen in your head afterwards. Relaxed and alone in your studio, you can reflect on all the things you've heard about your work. I find it echoes in my head long after the Crawl is over. When I'm painting, I think, yeah, people really liked this or that.

I think one of the difficulties of being an artist is spending a lot of time alone. You have to be a person that can tolerate a lot of solitude. And then, on the other hand, you must be able to chat easily with people and, beyond that, find a way to advocate for yourself in some way.

Chris: You referred to a coach.

Mary Anne: Yes, she's my friend. I find it hard to sell, so she asked me, "Do you think your art improves people's lives?" And I said, "For sure! Living with original art is very fulfilling." Then she taught me to reframe the idea and see that selling my art brought benefit to both my customer and me.

Leanne: I'd just like to clarify that I would encourage anyone to have a go at being an artist full-time through face-to-face sales, as I do. I fear that I may have been a little scary earlier. When faced with the choice of being represented by a gallery or being a less glamorous "market grunt," I chose the latter. Gallery representation is like a marriage; one needs to find oneself before committing to it, and my booth on Granville Island is the perfect way for me to finance the time I need to develop my painting.

Having said that, I wanted to warn artists that it is not an easy route. A while back, there was a week in which all of the vendors were really struggling to attract interest, and 2-D artists like me tend to suffer the most. I only had one week in the Market that month, so I really needed sales, but I had only made one or two small sales and I was looking at a loss. When Sunday arrived, after six ten-hour days of selling, I was not only exhausted but also disappointed and disheartened.

I spent a fair amount of energy tearing down not only my work, but also my ability to sell it. But at around hour 65, I chose to pick myself up, splash some water on my face and start again. When hour 67 came around, a lady returned to my table to take a closer look at some of my small pieces. With my renewed attitude, I started talking to her, and our conversation moved beyond sales to the passion I feel about my paintings. We discussed the challenges posed by Vancouver lighting and how, for me, it required a fresh approach to colour.

At the end of the conversation, she asked me to pack two 24" x 24" pieces up for her, each valued at over $1,000. Suddenly I had not just the money I needed, but I also had a friend. Selling may appear scary, but the rewards can be immense.

EPILOGUE

My sense of the importance of face-to-face sales is based on contact with numerous artists met through workshops, classes and coaching, as well as from the generous artists whose conversation is recorded here. I've learned that face-to-face sales can be a rich experience for prolific artists who produce work at reasonable price points, and who have a strong and outgoing personality.

As Leanne says, face-to-face sales are not for everybody. How you fare has a lot to do with how you interact with people. Leanne is an artist whose primary source of income is face-to-face sales. Selling directly to her customers is a constant experience for her, whereas for most of us, direct sales involve a smaller percentage of time.

When your primary face-to-face sales experience is involves a short-term and intense fair or festival, there is a glut of both customers and competition. Your challenge is to stand out. Events such as Vancouver's beloved Culture Crawl may involve tens of thousands of visitors, and for them, The Crawl is a generous buffet. There is so much to choose from that visitors will only stop for artists whose work or booth somehow stops the human traffic. Standing out can be a challenge, but one excellent and proven way to attract attention is to feature a demonstration.

At Richard Tetrault's studio, visitors can see his relief print blocks and see the developmental process of his work. His plates become props in conversations that arise out of the curiosity of his guests, and they afford him a comfortable opportunity to create relationships.

If you are an artist for whom self-advocacy or social engagement is a challenge, the demonstration idea can be particularly effective. I have seen artists engage a friend, relative or a professional salesperson to handle their sales at events, so that they can focus on working on their art as the demonstration. They are there to answer questions if need be, and to meet buyers, but they are freed from the primary responsibility for sales. If there is not room for an actual demonstration, an explanatory exhibit can engage customers.

A raffle can also build up your mailing list at open studio events. It is best to require visitors to ask for a raffle ticket, however, than to leave tickets out for visitors to complete. By making visitors ask for a ticket, you can engage them in a conversation while they provide their contact information. The end result of this process is a list of people with whom you have actually engaged and not merely a list of names.

If you conduct a raffle in order to build your mailing list, be sure to write to everyone on your list immediately after the event (and check local bylaws to ensure that your raffle is legal). Write to every non-winner, informing them in *positive terms* that they did not win. Give them information about the visual arts that they might value, and do not push sales or talk only about yourself. Make your correspondence about your customers and other artists. Focus on being friendly. Talk about other visual art activities that they might enjoy, and compliment them on attending the event at which you met. Later, when you have your next show or sale, send them promotional material.

Face-to-face interaction dominates the activities of many contemporary visual artists. You are required to talk to gallerists, customers, commissioners, patrons, parents, partners, juries and sponsors, and to convince them to *see* you. How we conduct ourselves at these meetings is crucial to our success. The most important thing is to think about the person you are addressing and not yourself.

Artists can be overly self-aware. Many are self-conscious; some are overly confident. And most people become more self conscious when meeting strangers; we tend to focus on ourself and on making a good impression. But if you want to succeed with direct face-to-face interactions, you must enjoy being focused on the customer, and on listening instead of speaking.

LINKS

Artists in our Midst: http://www.artistsinourmidst.com
Cheaper Show: http://thecheapershow.com
Circle Craft and Christmas Market: http://www.circlecraft.net
Eastside Culture Crawl: http://www.eastsideculturecrawl.com
Etsy: http://www.etsy.com
Flickr: http://www.flickr.com
Granville Island Public Market: http://www.granvilleisland.com
Main Street Art Drift: www.thedrift.ca
Twitter: http://twitter.com
Vancouver Farmers' Markets: http://www.eatlocal.org

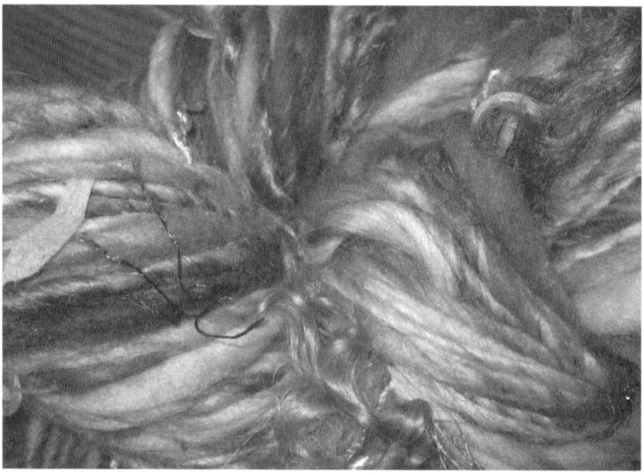

Photo by Barb Hunt

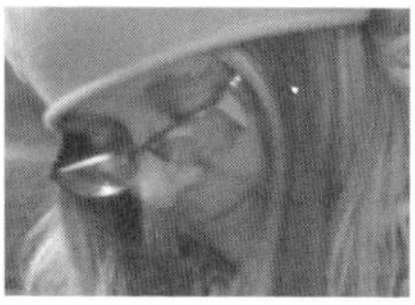

SHAWN O'HAGAN, 1950

Hand dyed, hand spun yarn

www.islandsweet.blogspot.com

2 Shawn O'Hagan

Adaptation: Shawn uses Etsy.com to reach international customers from her small hometown.

Date of interview: September 14, 2010

"I realized that Newfoundland wasn't my market. I knew that I needed to get my work off-island in order to make a living. And that's where Etsy came in."

— *Shawn O'Hagan*

PROLOGUE

The website Etsy.com has changed my view of online sales, at least for certain forms of hand-made, one-of-a-kind work—particularly 3D work. The Internet is an excellent medium for the promotional and informational aspects of visual art marketing, but it is not an effective sales medium for 2D work. Because it broadcasts in compromised colour and cannot effectively display tone and texture, it limits the customers' capacity to make informed decisions about artwork.

3-D, however, sells well on Etsy. But before all you fine artists turn to the next chapter, consider this: Regardless of your preferred medium or primary artistic product, Etsy can become a highly lucrative revenue stream for your creative practice. More than that, Etsy offers its members the option of participating in a richly resourceful online community where there is abundant shared learning about art and craft marketing.

Each term, teaching at Emily Carr University exposes me to a new cohort of emerging artists. One of my missions is to expand their sense of who they are – to encourage students (particularly those who wish to sell a lot of work) not to think of themselves as media specific artists (printmakers, painters, performance artists or sculptors), but as creative people with limitless options for fulfillment. Creative people bring novelty and innovation, not just to work that they call "art," but to everything they do.

The entrepreneurial creative person can have a career that accommodates work of curatorial integrity, as well as work that is market-friendly. Market-friendly work can be made with pride. With some forethought, Etsy can provide a highly affordable and accessible global market for the creative entrepreneur.

Shawn was a perfect choice to interview about her "store" on Etsy, not just because she is experienced with the site, but also because her story illustrates an aspect of business management that I greatly admire: The ability to be flexible and adapt to a changing environment (sociographic, geographic or economic). When she moved from the large art market of Toronto to a small coastal community in Newfoundland, she had to significantly change her creative practice. She had to make new products, find new markets, and learn e-marketing. Her story demonstrates an enviable and practical adaptability; she continues to thrive and adapt at a mature age.

Shawn has always been an artist, but many people of her generation are "retiring" into a creative practice to supplement their income or to fulfill a long-repressed creative muse. Many of these professional converts feel challenged by the technological demands of the Internet. Consequently, I value the opportunity to tell the story of someone from the Baby Boom generation who has successfully embraced technology and developed a healthy revenue stream by doing so.

I talked to Shawn by phone in her home in Corner Brook, Newfoundland.

INTERVIEW

When did you first get involved in making art?

I think my first memories involved *seeing* as an artist. Of course I didn't realize what was going on at the time, but when I look back, I have very vivid memories of being excited about color combinations and seeing life as though through a viewfinder.

Did your parents encourage your interest in art?

My mother was a commercial artist before she got married. My father had a nursery, and then he became a landscape architect and amateur photographer. I think they both encouraged the family about the value of creativity.

Did your teachers encourage your interest in art?

Yes. One in elementary school, and then in high school I had a wonderful teacher named Jane Buckle. Art was all I was interested in; it was a passion. I spent all my time in the library looking at art books; I grew up in Willowdale and then Thornhill, Ontario where there was not a lot of art around, so I found it in the library.

Ms Buckle only taught for one year. I became an art teacher because of her, but just like her, I only lasted one year teaching in the public school system. We both went on to make art.

You got your Bachelor of Education?

Yes. First I did a BFA at the University of Guelph and then got my art education degree at the University of Toronto. After that, I stayed home to raise the kids and didn't teach for ten years.

Were you making any art while you were raising the kids?

I was. I didn't think I was making important art though, because my education gave me a very narrow definition of what art was. I was doing a lot of sewing and knitting, and I illustrated a number of children's books. I started painting more seriously when my youngest child went into kindergarten. Then I started exhibiting some paintings. I was living in a small Newfoundland community at the time, then I moved to Corner Brook where I was able to get a job teaching at the junior-high school level. That was a disaster!

In the early Nineties, I went back to university and got my Masters of Fine Art in painting at the University of Waterloo. It was the first year that they had offered a Master's degree program, and the experience exposed me to a lot of new thought and new work. However, when I started working in the studio, I was painting less and less. Although my final thesis was on painting, I had become more interested in sculpture and textile work.

When I was finished my degree and came home, I did some painting, but I was more involved with textiles. Then, about ten years ago, I just decided I didn't want to paint anymore. I didn't really want to be making "Art" anymore. I wanted to be involved with simpler work—things that were more utilitarian and less expensive. For a time I was quilting, hooking, sewing and knitting, and selling my work in Newfoundland shops and craft fairs. But eventually, I wound up just knitting. I started making hats and scarves and things like that. Knitting in Newfoundland is very traditional, but with my background in painting and my good colour sense, I started doing quite well making funky stuff.

What does "funky" mean?

It means brightly coloured and heavily textured—a kind of quirkiness in the combinations of things I was knitting into the work. Traditional is very basic and plain. In the history of rural Newfoundland, everybody had their own sheep and dyed and spun their own wool. Everybody knit because they had to. It was the same with hooked mats. These things—the knitted and the hooked wares—were not thought of as art objects; they were essential items for the home. People just kept doing things the traditional way, sticking to traditional patterns.

So what you were doing was unique. Were you aware that you would be creating a new market?

Oh, absolutely! I realized that knitting was what I wanted to. Then about three years ago, when I was in New York, I found a skein of yarn in a shop called Purl Soho. I looked at it and thought, "I want to knit with yarn like this!" But I couldn't afford to buy it and knit products to sell if I wanted to make any profit at all. If I did that, the price became too high. So I learned how to spin wool. I went to Nova Scotia for a week to learn basic techniques and then continued learning on my own. I started knitting using my own yarn and then I started selling skeins. But in Newfoundland—because knitting is traditional and because everybody's grandmother knits—it's very hard to sell a skein of yarn for $40 when you can buy a pair of exquisite hand-knit socks for $16. I realized that Newfoundland wasn't my market. I knew that I needed to get my work off-island in order to make a living. And that's where Etsy came in.

I love your blog and how you display your skeins with photographs of your sources of inspiration.

I think my approach to my knitting and sales stems from my painting background. This morning I was thinking about a place on the northern peninsula of the west coast of Newfoundland called Shallow Bay. It has the most incredible sand dunes with little wisps of grasses growing through the sand. So I did a skein called Sand Dunes of Shallow Bay. It's mostly a beige/bone colour, with cut up strips of novelty yarns spun into it. It's got green strips of very shaggy commercial yarn, plus a bit of blue, brown and black. I always start a skein with an idea or a feeling. For example, the other day as I was grabbing handfuls of the loose pieces of yarn I keep in the studio, I started thinking about New York and the barrage of colour and light you see in Times Square. Every time I go to that city, I get so inspired. And so I made a skein with some really thin sparkly fibres to make a Times Square skein.

If these skeins are all unique, what if a customer wants more similar skeins?

I can make some skeins that are very similar, but because I do all my own dyeing quite intuitively, it is hard for me to replicate the exact colours.

What can a person do with one skein?

Most of my skeins weigh between three and four ounces—with that much yarn, you can make a long scarf or a hat. Or what you can do is buy a skein, and then go through your supply of unused yarn and mix them together for a larger project. There are all sorts of possibilities for customers.

I also sell smaller skeins that I sell in a package with patterns on postcards, plus wooden knitting needles. I paint the tops of the needles with colours to match the colours in the yarn. That's my latest project. The package is $40, and with that, you can knit your own scarf or pair of fingerless gloves.

Are people commissioning from you?

I do commissions all the time. Recently, I made a large throw for a woman who had seen a skein of my yarn in Toronto last winter. She was redecorating her bedroom and wanted to use the colours I'd used in a piece she saw that I had sold. So I dyed up a whole lot of yellow and grey wool and took photos of them and sent them to her. She liked what she saw, and so I spun a very large skein pulling in other yarns and made the throw for her.

I recently did a throw for a woman from Los Angeles who had been buying quite a bit of work from me over the last couple of years off Etsy. She wanted a shawl with autumn colours, so I did a skein with the colours she described to me and then we went through the same back-and-forth process to fill her order.

How did you find out about Etsy?

I read about it in the *Globe and Mail*. I knew that I needed a web-presence, but I wasn't very computer-savvy. I knew that it would be difficult to get someone to set up a web page, and I wanted something that was very interactive—something I could be adding to every day because I really hate websites that never change. Also, I was concerned about the expense of a website.

Then I heard about blogs and started one with the idea that I would write about what was inspiring me and what I was making. Then, almost immediately, I found out about Etsy. It was just perfect. Instead of people having to stumble upon my blog, Etsy delivered the whole world to me.

So you set up a shop on Etsy?

Yes, it's a very simple thing to do. I had no trouble at all setting it up.

What is involved with setting up a shop?

First, I joined to be a buyer and to get to know the site. I started buying yarn from other sellers to see how things worked. I had to set up a PayPal account first, and then I set up my shop called Island Sweet. That meant, basically, choosing a name (and I already had one that nobody else was using), and a photo to use as a banner. Etsy takes you through the process, step by step; I was able to get through it very easily.

And if you're technically challenged, you can hire someone or find a friend to do the technical part, right?

Absolutely. I helped a number of my friends who now have Etsy shops.

And how much time a week do you spend online and dealing with orders?

First thing each morning, I work on my blog and then go to Etsy to add one or two new items. Or, if I'm not adding new items, I "renew" previously posted pieces because within an hour of posting work, it can wind up on page three or four of people's searches. By the end of the day, it's likely buried on page twenty and Etsy has found that people don't tend to go past page three of searches. I "renew" about three or four times a day when my store is active. It costs twenty cents each time you post a new item or renew an item, so I'm spending between one and two dollars a day on Etsy.

What is really important with Etsy is that you treat it as a part-time job. You have to keep your shop current by adding new products all the time. Right now, I'm pulling back on Etsy because I have a big show coming up in Toronto and I have a hard time making enough product for everything at once. But I am serious about the shop; I only slow down when I absolutely have to. When I slow down on Etsy, it's for as short a time as possible.

You can temporarily take your store offline?

Yes. You just click a button that says "vacation mode," and put a little announcement saying that you are going to be gone until… and you put in the date. They've got it worked out so it's very easy to use.

Your marketing costs are only $10 a week! That's pretty reasonable.

And it's for the world! I'm selling in Europe and Australia and most of the sales I am getting are from the United States.

On a good week, what kind of volume of sales would you enjoy?

It's hard to say. I've had my shop up for two and a half years but it is not always open. Since I started though, I have made just over 250 sales. Last week I sold seven pieces of knitwear, so that's about, maybe, $500 to $600. But once I went three weeks without a sale.

What other strategies are important on Etsy?

If you're not selling, chances are you're not putting enough time in. I was looking at some statistics this morning, and there are four hundred thousand sellers on Etsy right now. One key to having a successful shop is carefully choosing your "tags." Tags are words you use to describe your work; you're allowed up to fourteen tags for every item you put up on your shop. For example, this morning I put up a skein, and my first tag was "supplies," and then I added "hand spun," "yarn," "wool," "skein," etc. And it's a really good idea to tag your colour. Another way to attract Etsy shoppers is through their "Treasuries" feature. Treasuries are posts of collections made by buyers or sellers who assemble items they like; Etsy only allows a limited number of Treasuries at one time, so it's kind of competitive. My work is often in Treasuries, so when people go to Etsy and they visit Treasuries for ideas, they see my work. They might not buy it, but they see it and the name of my shop. Then, when they are ready, they may come back and buy something.

Do you tag all your emails with a link to your Etsy store to advertise it?

Absolutely. I've got my Etsy store linked to my blog, and a few months ago I joined Facebook. I put an Etsy item on my Facebook homepage every day—either the newest item I've done or one that I've renewed. Plus it's linked, so they can go to directly to my Etsy shop or my blog from Facebook. It's all interconnected. I just started on Twitter, but I don't really know how to use it yet. I just know that, again, it's free and can extend awareness. Living in a remote community, I feel it's important to get out there and on the Internet as much as possible.

When you get an order, what are the fulfillment demands like?

When you list an item, you adjust its cost to cover shipping. For an $80 cowl that costs $6 to ship, the buyer pays $86 into PayPal.

Then you get the email notice from PayPal?

Yes. Etsy tells you that you've sold something, and then PayPal confirms receipt of payment. Then I contact the buyer—not everybody does this, but I think this is really important to make a personal connection. I want them to know that they're buying from an individual, not a company. I will write to thank them for their purchase and to tell them that I'll get their purchase into the mail following day. I let them know, if they are American, that it will take up to three weeks if things get stopped at customs, or that otherwise, it should be there in about ten days. It works very smoothly, and I find that people don't mind if things take longer because I live in such a remote place. People can be understanding and sympathetic as long as you keep in contact with them.

How do you get your money from PayPal?

It accumulates, and then I transfer it into my bank account. It's unbelievable! And I can do it in Canadian or American dollars. And oh, that's another thing I should mention, I do the Toronto One of a Kind Show, and a lot of people who have bought from me there are moving to Etsy now to continue to buy my work. I have noticed many more Canadians buying from me in the last six months—I think the States is really reeling. I had some regular American customers that were buying often that aren't buying anymore. But with the new Canadian sales, it's balancing.

Have you experienced any problems with the site?

When I have, it has usually been because a buyer doesn't know how to use Etsy properly. They will buy one of my items and then the payment won't come through. So if I get a sale notice from Etsy but no notice comes from PayPal confirming payment, I will write to the buyer and say, "Thanks for buying my work. When your PayPal payment comes through, I'll get it right into the mail." I write something like that to nudge them, and they often write back and say, "Oh! I didn't know I hadn't paid!" It's nearly always new buyers who have trouble with Etsy.

And there’s another thing that's amazing about Etsy. I have made some very good friends through the site who live in the States. I think that I may have bought something from them originally, but then we started doing trades and became friends. I've even got a standing invitation to visit New Mexico and stay with a woman who has a yarn shop there with an apartment attached to it. She’s invited me to come and stay with her. We write to each other and follow each other's blogs now, and we met through Etsy.

So Etsy is a virtual community, like Facebook, but for artists.

Absolutely. Often I will see something I really like in someone else's shop, so I'll write and say, "I just love your work.” And it's really nice when people write to me in the same way—I love having other artists commenting on my work. I definitely feel like I am part of a community.

They also have what they call “teams” on Etsy. I belong to a fibre-art team, and it's very active; it’s a Yahoo chat group. When I first got involved with Etsy I was quite involved with chatting, but I’m not so much anymore. I still get a summary every day about what's being said, and if there's something I'm interested in, I'll go in and post a comment. Joining a Team is a really good way to get started on the site, and it’s a good way to get advice from other Etsy sellers. Etsy doesn't feel competitive. People readily share their experience and are helpful.

EPILOGUE

Shawn has become master of her self-made digital universe, and she has done it while in her sixties. Take heart from her assurances that the process is relatively simple, and take note of her process: She was a buyer first, before she opened her store. Also, she recognized the value of becoming part of the community, building bridges to other members by buying or trading work and by participating in the chat room.

Obviously, the uniqueness, the visual impact and the artistry of her work are primary reasons for Shawn’s success. Her career has benefited from her education and her trained artist’s eye. But her decisions to develop a product line that is light and easy to ship, and to take full advantage of technology, have also been pivotal to her success.

Her appealing blog serves a valuable informational and promotional function. Her posts fill her customers with confidence about the integrity of their purchase; they not only buy a product, they also get a related story rich in insight into her inspiration and process.

Shawn followed her creative instincts through several different media. Her story demonstrates a career-long curiosity and facility with change—traits that served her well when she relocated to Corner Brook. Her move did not stop her creative career; she adapted. She took on the challenge of changing her practice with a positive and pragmatic outlook. I find her story inspirational.

It's worth mentioning that a prime value of Etsy is in its capacity to earn artists almost the full retail price of their work. Artists who want to make a business of their work normally have to base their business's profitability on wholesale pricing, so an outlet such as Etsy that takes little commission (3.5%) presents a wonderful opportunity.

If, however, you are selling work wholesale to retail outlets, you owe it to these vendors to restrict Internet sales to markets outside their service areas. They will appreciate that, so be sure to tell them what you are doing. It will strengthen your relationship with these valuable partners.

LINKS

Etsy: www.etsy.com
Facebook: www.facebook.com
Island Sweet: www.islandsweet.etsy.com
Purl Soho: www.purlsoho.com
One of a Kind Show: www.oneofakindshow.com
PayPal: www.paypal.com
Twitter: http://twitter.com

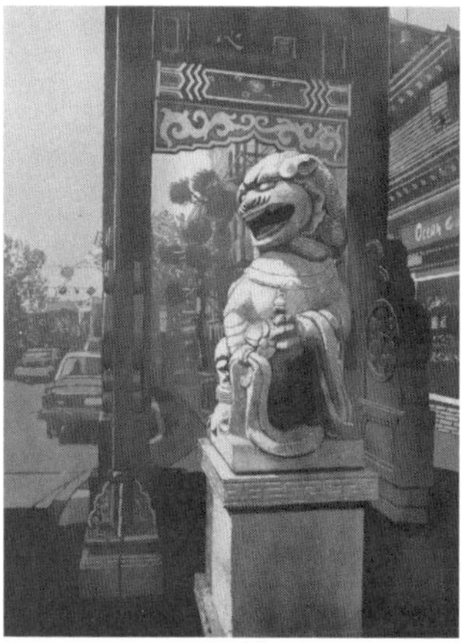

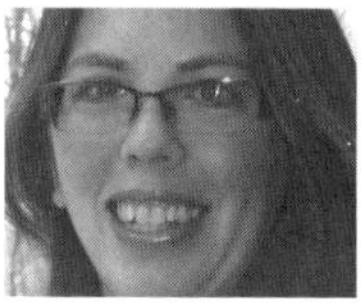

LESLIE REDHEAD, 1972
Unity; poured watercolour
2010; 21" x 29"

http://leslieredhead.com

3 Leslie Redhead

Self-Promotion: Leslie has a dynamic and effective online presence; her blog is a perfect professional model.

Date of interview: October 13, 2010

"I [blog] about things I'm working on or about getting into a show—it isn't about a new painting every time. And I try to make time every week for Facebook and Twitter. I am really enjoying it. I've had people from all over the world commenting on my work."

— *Leslie Redhead*

PROLOGUE

Leslie's artistic practice is an excellent model for emerging or transitioning artists. The diversity of her creative output, her involvement with her community and her talent with a difficult medium are vital factors of her success, but it is her dynamic online presence that so impressed me. Leslie's blog reveals the depths and diversity of her talent and that she loves what she does. I experienced a sense of joy and energy as I read it.

When people buy art, they want to know the artist. Through her blog, Leslie provides the world with the opportunity to have a relationship with her. Blogs are fabulous marketing tools for artists. Many artists in this book have developed very effective blogs to support their practice, but I chose to focus on Leslie's for the following reasons:

1. THE TITLE: Leslie's name is her brand, and it's appropriate that her name is the first two words of her blog's title (too bad we can't all have a name so memorable). The third word of her blog's title is her medium, letting visitors know immediately what she does.
2. THE BACKGROUND: The background is clean and simple. It is not cluttered; it doesn't compete with the important foreground material. Also, being a splash of water, it is appropriate given her preference for water media.
3. THE QUOTATION: The simplicity of the quote by Edward Hopper says, perhaps more eloquently than Leslie can, why she paints. And by quoting a well-known and respected painter, she suggests her professional level or aspiration. Linking her name with his may help give customers faith in her work.
4. THE STRUCTURE: Access to her products and services is provided through tags that stretch in a band near the top of her blog page. The tags provide visitors with easy access to her portrait, poured watercolour and landscape galleries, or with information on her workshops. She also has separate galleries for her site-specific work from Chinatown and Spain. The tags advertise the diversity of her practice; the structure of her site tells us she was thinking of the convenience of customers when she built it.
5. THE WORKSHOPS: By doing workshops, Leslie meets many student artists who can become customers and/or word-of-mouth advertisers.

By offering workshops, she becomes a social resource and increases her visibility in her community.

6. THE EVENT PROMOTION: The right hand side of her blog is a vertical list of resources. On the day I visited, on the top right was an image linked to a downloadable guide for the Annual Oak Bay Artists' Studio Tour happening a few weeks later. By putting the guide in so prominent a position, Leslie demonstrates a commitment to her community and provides visitors with information about the next opportunity to meet her and see her work.
7. THE PHOTO: A photo of Leslie is always visible on her site. This personalizes the site, helps visitors form an attachment and allows them to identify her at live events. It guides the focus of visitors to the artist and not only to the work.
8. THE CALENDAR: The calendar offers visitors immediate information on accessibility to Leslie, her work and her classes.
9. THE GADGETS: If you scroll down her homepage, on the right side of the screen, you will see gadgets that provide:
    a. Links to other sites where her work is featured, giving viewers confidence in her work.
    b. Her lengthy list of links to other artists indicates her involvement with her community, supports her peer artists and furthers the education of her site visitors. (Presumably, the artists listed on her site provide links to Leslie on their websites.)
    c. A thumbprint version of a book she has done with a link to Blurb.com where you can buy it.
    d. A link to her store on Etsy, helping to facilitate sales.
    e. The list of her followers instills consumer confidence.
    f. A link to her Facebook page, allowing fans to stay more actively in touch.
    g. A fun map that allows people to indicate where they live shows visitors that Leslie has "fans" all over the world.
10. THE VISIBLE PRICING: Leslie's home page changes regularly. On the days I visited, several images of her work were always visible on the home page, priced at very accessible prices. Not all her works were priced, but those that were give visitors a clear understanding of

Leslie's price range. What better way is there to garner customer interest than proudly advertising meritorious work at accessible prices?

11. THE POSTS: Her posts are interesting and short; short is important on the web. They include images and are hyperlinked to further information where the work is for sale (for the convenience of customers).
12. THE LINKS: Just like Amazon.com, Leslie provides "customer-service" links at the foot of her posts. Her "You might also like this" links recommend works for sale, based on the image or story on her blog or site that visitors have chosen to view.

I talked by telephone with Leslie from her home in Victoria, BC.

INTERVIEW

Did you become involved in the visual arts very early in your life?

I studied visual arts in high school, but I ended up studying zoology at Brigham Young University. I'm American; I was raised in Washington, D.C., where I could spend every other weekend at the National Gallery. I loved living there.

I was nine years old when my mother took me to see the Rodin exhibit, and there were naked statues of men. I'd never seen anything like that, and I was shocked that my mother had taken me there. She explained to me that it was art and that she wanted me to learn more about it.

I spent my summers at a high school for the arts; a teacher of mine suggested that I go, and my parents were totally supportive. It was 9:00 to 3:00 every day, and we drew like crazy. We went on field trips around Baltimore and D.C. and drew everything we saw—and we had homework. It was very intensive.

Were you doing any painting while you were in college?

I did in my freshman (first) year, but everyone said that you couldn't earn a living making art. Then I met a professor that did scientific illustrations. My parents were teachers, so I knew I didn't want to teach, but this professor opened my eyes. He was a marine biologist who did scientific illustrations; meeting him made me think that I could combine biology and art, so I ended up switching my major to zoology my sophomore (second) year.

You got a Bachelor of Science?

Yes, I did. And I got married about the same time.

And got Redhead as your last name?

Yes, that's my husband's last name.

Does he have red hair?

No, he doesn't. And I don't think people take me seriously because of my name. But you know what? Once they meet me, they never forget!

Did you get back to painting after graduation?

I became a zoo keeper at an aviary. And then we decided to start a family. My husband was still in school, and because I was pregnant while I was working in the aviary, I ended up just hating it. So I started wondering about what I could do, and realized that I wanted to get back to being more creative. I started taking night classes at the local community college in graphic design and illustration, but then we moved to Boston so my husband could go to graduate school. In Boston, I started waking up at 5:00 in the morning to paint.

Why so early in the morning?

Once my daughter was born, I couldn't get any creative work done during the day. So I would get up before her, and I'd paint for an hour or two.

Were you painting with a mind to earning a living?

My goal was to be able to earn a supplemental income while I was at home with my children. And I was trying to improve my skills; I was painting birds at that time. Then I had another child, so it wasn't until 2002 when I really got back to painting. And then, in 2003, I met Beth Patterson. She's with the American Watercolour Society and she writes for Watercolour Magazine, and she started mentoring me. A mutual friend was her boyfriend, and he told me that she took private students every now and again and that he could introduce me to her.

Were you paying for the mentoring?

At first I was. I went in as a student, but then she ended up giving me a lot of free advice. I wanted to do watercolour portraits, so she taught me how to get started—how to get into shows and how to get known in the community. She introduced me to the work of some of the well-known watercolourists, gently pushing me to reach a higher level with my work.

She got me involved with the North East Watercolour Society. It's one of the oldest watercolour societies in the US. That's where she had me get started. I was in two of their shows, including one national show. And, while I was in Boston, I was asked to teach at one of the art centres. Then we ended up moving again.

To where, this time?

To Victoria. That was in 2006, and I couldn't do anything the first year because I wasn't able to work legally, being an American. My husband is from Victoria, that's why we came back. When we got here, it was the first year that my kids were in school so I could focus on painting again. I got into *Splash Ten*. It's a series of books called *Splash: The Best of Watercolour*. It comes out every other year. Right after we moved to Victoria, one of my pieces was in it.

And why is that significant to you?

Because I was suddenly in the company of all these wonderful watercolour artists I'd been studying. It gave me confidence, and I could use being in the book for marketing. And that same year, the watercolour instructor at the local recreation centre left. Somebody on the board knew that I painted in watercolour, so I got a call, showed them my work, and they invited me to take over the class. I wound up teaching three classes.

Do you still teach?

Yes, and I'm probably best known for teaching. Victoria's a really odd market. It's hard to sell here because everyone's an artist and/or on fixed income. Everyone is—or wants to be—an artist; they don't want to buy art. So I changed how I work. I used to do watercolour portraits, but portraits don't do well here, so I put my time into my classes and teach from two-to-five classes a week during the school year. You don't get paid well at community centres, but success isn't always monetary. Teaching helps to bring about other things.

Give me an idea of who your students are.

The median age is probably 55 and the students are largely female. They're an educated bunch, mostly nurses and teachers. A lot are retired.

Great contacts for your mailing list! Do you stay in touch with them all?

Yes. They like coming to my demonstrations and other classes that I teach. I teach at Painter's Lodge and Ocean Wilderness Inn on Vancouver Island. They enjoy watching me paint, and I always fill my classes.

Do you find it easy to teach and promote yourself?

I would say that I had to learn this. One of the reasons I started painting was so that I didn't have to interact much with people. But then I realized that I had to learn how to do it. Teaching came rather naturally, maybe because my parents are teachers, but I also have had some very good friends who have helped me learn how to get better at it. Plus, a person I met who hires artist-teachers, told me to take a workshop from Lian Zhen. She told me that I needed to learn about teaching from him because he was her best instructor.

And what did you learn from him?

I learned to speak in a way that beginners can understand. While he teaches, he always makes sure everyone understands what he is talking about. If they look confused, he backs up and explains things again. He's very good at reading his audience; he isn't like many instructors who approach their teaching intuitively and often don't know how to explain what they are doing. Inexperienced teachers sometimes focus on themselves instead of their students.

You belong to the Federation of Canadian Artists (FCA). Do you submit to their shows?

Not as much any more. I used to. I don't because I have changed my approach to selling, due to the decline of the economy.

How has your approach changed?

I no longer do watercolour portraits. Instead, I do very small pieces that are more affordable and that I can do quickly. Plus, I can do them as demonstrations in my classes.

That's brilliant! You're getting paid to create work that you then sell.

Well, not only that, but teaching also pays me to learn. About a year ago, I decided that I needed to improve the way I was painting water. So I thought, why don't I teach it? This year I'm teaching courses on skies because I want to improve my skies.

And you're selling on Etsy?

I haven't made a lot of sales through Etsy, but I have found that people find me through the site, and then they link to my website where they've found something that they like. I sold a couple of large pieces that way.

You're Twittering and on Facebook?

Yes, but using the Internet really started with my blog. Since I'm doing small work now, I have the time to blog. I try to post three times a week in order to keep it fresh and exciting. I post about things I'm working on or about getting into a show—it isn't about a new painting every time. And I try to make time every week for Facebook and Twitter. I am really enjoying it. I've had people from all over the world commenting on my work.

And do your students link up to your Facebook and Twitter accounts?

Sometimes I post things on my blog for my students to work on during the week. They go to my blog and see my demonstration or check my calendar to see when I'm teaching, and where.

Do you participate in any fairs at all, where there are direct personal sales?

I do the Moss Street Paint-In each summer. Even though sales are low, I meet people and get them interested in my classes. I have a sign that says, "I teach classes, please ask me," and I have an email list for people to sign. I also have bookmarks that I make that have one of my paintings on the front, and information about my workshops and my web address on the back. And they always have my blog address on them, as well as my phone number and the names of the galleries that carry my work.

And you've made a book through the Blurb.com website?

It's called *Leslie Redhead: The Life of an Artist.* And inside, I do a quick little original illustration, usually a flower, to personalize each one.

Do you sell it at twice the manufacturing cost?

My book is not cost effective. I did it in 2008 and I've probably sold about twenty-five of them. I sell them for $50 and it costs me probably about $43 to make by the time I've paid for shipping. I don't sell them any more really, because it's my old work. I ended up dropping the price on Blurb and selling directly from their website, so now they're not personalized, but I don't have to pay shipping either.

You've got so many things going on, and the energy you put into your life is very successfully transmitted through your blog.

I really enjoy doing it all and, as I said, it's not always the monetary return that matters. If I had to support my family, I couldn't do it. I'm doing it primarily so that I can be at home with my kids. A woman approached me last week. She's started a company that prints images on the cover of notebooks. The book she made using one of my images looks fantastic; the books are a new item for me to sell. They give me another way to get my artwork out there, and again, I can personalize them. So, if you see a painting of mine that you like, I can have her put it on a sketchbook or make a notebook for you.

Do you make cards?

I stopped making cards because they took up too much time, there was too much money involved, and they hardly ever sold. Every artist sells greeting cards. I decided I'd rather spend that time doing one of my hundred-dollar paintings.

So after only three years, your career in Victoria seems to be doing well.

At times it's been hard. There have been lots of times that I wished I made more money. But you know what? I've met my goal to be home with my kids.

And when they leave home, you'll step into a thriving creative practice.

That's what I'm hoping for.

EPILOGUE

Leslie was a stranger when I dialled her number; she was a friend when I hung up. Her warmth and energy serve her well in a business that can be so focused on inter-personal sales. The energy I sensed from her website reflects the exuberance with which she embraces her life and her creative practice. As she says, she is having fun and accomplishing her goals. Her practicality, adaptability and talent have led to considerable success in three short years. The financial support of her husband is underwriting the development of her business, which could grow into a viable enterprise by the time her children leave home.

Leslie is entrepreneurial, so I am confident that her practice, already operating at a level to which many artists aspire, will eventually sustain her. She teaches, which is an excellent way to earn career-related income, and she was wise to pursue training in pedagogy and to recognize that the focus of her classes must always be on the students' experience. Also, she knows her market. She lives in one of the densest communities of artists in Canada; a city with a relatively mature median age. Her smartest career move, given these conditions, was her choice to work small in order to sell low.

She has embraced and mastered technology, and she is wise to have done so. Although the web is not a great medium for sales of 2-D artwork, it is an invaluable tool with which to maximize many professional activities: Mailing list management, learning software, buying supplies, networking, self-promotion, research, etcetera. Leslie has created a very effective web presence that reflects the energy, talent and diversity of her practice.

BLOG HOSTING

Google this question: "How to make a blog," to see the amount of information available to you if you want to start a blog. My own blogs were easy to make and are fun to sustain. Two of the most popular sites offering free blog hosting and training are:

- Blogger: www.blogger.com
- WordPress: http://wordpress.org

LINKS

American Watercolor Society: www.americanwatercolorsociety.com
Federation of Canadian Artists (FCA): http://artists.ca
Lian Zhen: www.lianspainting.com
Moss Street Paint In: http://aggv.ca/events/gallery-paint-in
North East Watercolor Society: www.northeastws.com
Ocean Wilderness Inn: www.oceanwildernessinn.com
The Painter's Lodge: www.painterslodge.com

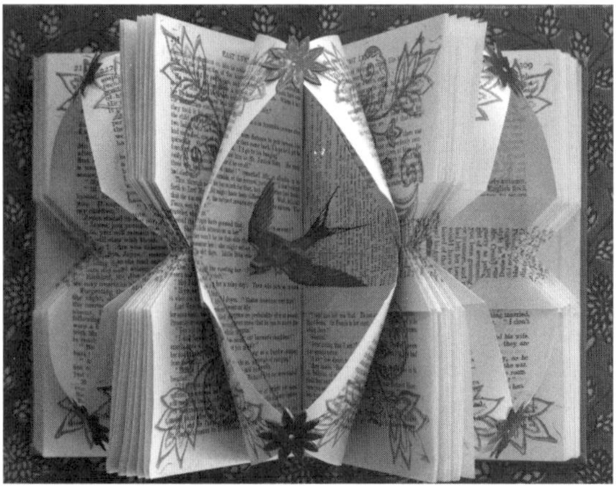

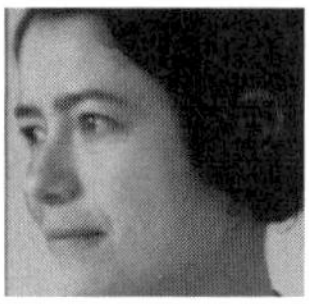

RACHAEL ASHE, 1972
Looking for Signs of a Safe Return Home; altered book; 2009; 8" x 10" framed

http://rachaelashe.com

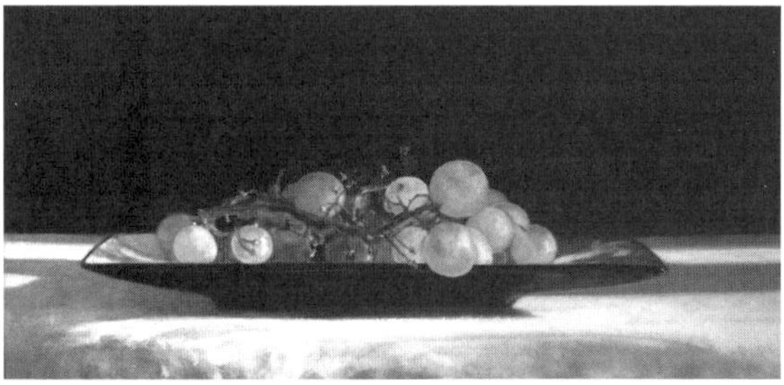

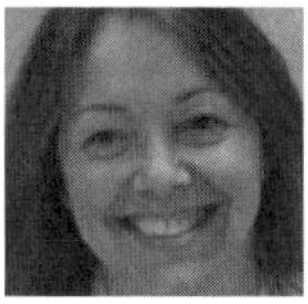

KRISTINE PATON, 1954
Sweetness & Light; acrylic on canvas 2005; 12" x 24"

http://www.paton-place.com

4 Rachael Ashe / Kristine Paton

Communications: Kristine and Rachael use online marketing services to manage their communications.

Dates of interviews:
Rachael, October 21, 2010
Kristine, October 29, 2010

"If you're taught properly to use social media tools, you know that it's important to use your personal voice, and not just be promoting yourself all the time. Be a human being. Promote other people and other things, not just yourself. "

— *Rachael Ashe, on MailChimp*

"It's so much more professional looking than using regular email. I just love the look of it. I can upload my images so easily into their templates, and I like the consistent look it gives to my communications."

— *Kristine Paton, on Constant Contact*

PROLOGUE

Perhaps nothing is more valuable to an artist than a large mailing list. Knowing the right people, and knowing a *lot* of people, have always been vital factors in the professional development of a successful artist.

Art galleries are not much different than artists in this regard. After all, art galleries are really nothing more than large empty rooms. When they are fully installed with a show, they are still empty rooms; nothing that you see for sale inside is owned by the gallery. The real value of the gallery is its mailing list; its list of past and potential buyers whose taste in art is shaped and fulfilled by the director of the gallery.

Artists who are not represented by a gallery need to find their own buyers and, during the span of their career, must develop their own (extensive) mailing list. The growth of your creative practice will be determined by your ability to solicit sales from the contacts on your list and, if you are successful at direct sales, it can often lead to gallery representation later in your career. Gallery directors value artists who have a sizeable mailing list.

Unrepresented artists are focused on direct sales by default, and although there are innumerable rewards that can come from success with direct sales (see chapter one), many artists fear the challenge of sales. Direct sales, however, have never been easier for artists. Thanks to the technological revolution brought about by the personal computer, the Internet and software developers, more artists are selling work without a gallery or its commission. The bulk of direct sales originate with the artist's list.

As a teacher of professional development for visual artists, I advocate the value and methodology of direct sales. But teaching students how to manage their personal sales in a curriculum that is far more focused on aesthetics, is a serious challenge. Learning how to write compelling sales copy requires a course, not an hour or two in a class, and trying to teach the critical skills involved with data management is even more challenging in the time available. But now there are two valuable web-based communication services that can do all that.

MailChimp and Constant Contact are two sites that I value greatly because of their simple accessibility and the complexity of the services they offer self-employed professionals. Each is a "one-stop-shop" of communication management services that are ideal for artists. Initially, both sites require that you input all the e-addresses of your existing mailing list before being able to take advantage of their services, but depending on the program you use, you may be able to upload all your addresses from your existing e-address book. The variety of services these sites offer and the results you can obtain are substantial.

Both sites offer similar services; which one is right for you is a subjective decision, but what is certain is that both sites offer services that *many* artists need. They both provide users with a highly professional communications veneer—check them out before you choose which one to use. Or, as I often advise, use the same service as someone you know. When you do that, you have an experienced fellow site user with whom you feel comfortable enough to ask for free advice or assistance.

I have spent slightly more time looking at the Constant Contact site. It is strong in training. You can visit its Learning Centre and take advantage of the site's many resources, or you can look under Industry Best Practices and click on the link to Local Learning. When you do that, the site gives you information about the live training and network sessions closest to where you live.

Both sites have video lessons, templates and examples for you to study and consider. The more research and learning you do about direct sales and mailing list use, the better your outcomes will be. Like the Etsy site (see chapter two), these two sites are much more than the services they sell—they are interactive online communities. Members can develop relationships with other members, trading ideas and hints. And, new services are added as the collective experience of the site's members drive its evolution.

These sites offer you services that are hard for you to emulate on your own. In addition to communication services, they provide you with valuable statistics about your list and its members that increase in complexity and sophistication the more you use the site.

These sites can tell you how many people read the communications you distribute. They provide convenient services allowing your mailing list members to easily remove themselves from your list or to link to your other online resources. Constant Contact offers professional consultation services as part of its fees, and they brag about how quickly they respond to your requests for assistance.

MailChimp is free if you have a list smaller than 1,000 names, and your free status allows you to send up to 6,000 messages per month—way more than enough. Constant Contact has a free trial period, but costs a modest $15 monthly thereafter. Fifteen dollars a month is $180 per year or the equivalent of your commission on the sale of a single $360 dollar artwork—a bargain for such a rich variety of professional direct marketing services and support!

To know more about these sites and their services, I talked to Rachael Ashe and Kristine Paton by telephone. Rachael is based in Vancouver; Kristine lives in Cowichan Bay, B.C.

INTERVIEW: RACHAEL USES MAILCHIMP

Do you remember when you first got involved in art?

I've always been artistic. Art was part of the curriculum, and I was always drawn to it. At first it was drawing and painting, and then I got into photography. I'm originally from Brampton, Ontario, and I took two courses in photography when I was in high school. I learned the basics of camera and darkroom techniques and that got me really interested in photography.

I knew I wanted to make art as a career, so I decided to focus on photography rather than doing illustration work or animation, which were things I had considered. I felt I didn't have the drawing skills for a career in art, so I went to Humber College for a two-year photography course. It was a very commercial program—it was not artistic at all—but it did provide me with a good technical and commercial base. I had to develop my creative side on my own.

What happened when you finished that program?

Initially, I was kind of at a loss about what to do because it is really hard to get into photography. I ended up working at a portrait studio and photo lab for a short time, and didn't really enjoy working there. Then I started volunteering at a gallery in Brampton, and eventually I got hired there. It exposed me to a lot of on-the-job learning in the visual arts. I worked with other galleries and museums as well, and learned things like how to mat and frame, and about how to do research and install shows. It was a great education for me on how to be an artist and how galleries are run. I was there, on and off, for several years.

And then?

Then I moved to Toronto, and took training in digital tools such as Quark Express, Photoshop and Illustrator, and I studied a bit about web design. That led me to concentrate on Photoshop and to becoming a digital artist and photographer. I became the in-house digital re-toucher for a photography studio, with a focus on shooting stock photography. But, just before doing that, I did an internship at the Textile Museum of Canada, working on a project to photograph and digitize their permanent collection. That internship led to a permanent part-time job at the textile museum for almost four years.

And then?

I gave up my jobs and my apartment and went traveling for six months to New Zealand, Japan and Germany. And when I came back home to Toronto, I had to start my life over again. It was really hard to find a job, and eventually I just felt like I didn't fit in there anymore. So I decided to move to Vancouver, on instinct really, in 2004.

Until I moved to Vancouver, I'd made art on the side. But working for the gallery in Brampton had earned me a place in a show there. That experience got me interested in entering juried shows and having little solo shows. Moving to Vancouver resulted in me doing a lot more work.

Were you working in Vancouver or just making art?

I decided I didn't want to work in a creative field anymore. I decided I would get whatever kind of job I could, and do my art for myself, rather than try to do it for a living. I worked in a lot of administrative jobs, but I got involved with a meet-up group through Flickr.com, and that led to going out to do photo walks with members of the group. Eventually, I became the group organizer.

The Flickr group was photography-based?

Yes. It got me shooting regularly and really developing my eye. Being part of the group re-ignited my passion for photography and for trying different things, like using toy cameras and being much more experimental. I started showing more, and getting published in magazines—trying to get my work "out there." It's so important to develop discipline with your work, because if you're not doing it regularly, you don't develop a flow.

And you started working in other media?

I'd always shot film; that's how I learned photography. But once I started shooting with the digital camera, I needed something to do that would be more hands-on again. So I started doing collage. I made goals: To do collage in a sketchbook every week, and to do a photographic self-portrait every week. It gave me a nice balance between shooting digital self-portraits and working on them in Photoshop, and having hands-on play with paper and objects in my sketchbook. And that led to doing altered books.

Working with books was an idea I'd had for quite a few years. On a trip to Portland in 2007, I saw an artist who'd done illustrations inside old books. They were magical, and they inspired me to try something similar with my photographs. Using books to make art had been in the back of my mind for a long time. Then, in September 2009, I came across a book called *New Directions in Altered Books*, and it was a revelation of things you could do with books. So, for the past year, I've been altering books and doing a series of photographs of women.

Are you still using Flickr as a social media tool for developing your mailing list contacts?

Flickr is less of a social media tool now, and it's more of an archive. Flickr's evolved a lot over the last several years and people don't use it the way they used to.

Do you use Facebook then?

I use Twitter a lot, and Facebook less. I use every web tool I can to put my work out there and to connect with people. Because of Flickr, I've had a gallery in LA contact me, and sometimes people have contacted me to use my work as stock imagery.

But you're not much of a Facebook person?

I do use it. I set up my profile and artist pages there, and if I have an event coming up, I post it on Facebook. It's good to use all these different services.

Why Twitter?

It's more immediate, and it's more of a conversation, in a way. It's more of an open platform than Facebook. Yesterday, I did a search of my name on Twitter (I check every once in a while). I found that people hadn't referenced my Twitter account directly, but people had used my name in conjunction with information about my altered books. I could search my name and see that they had done this, and then I could write back to them and thank them for sharing my work.

How would you describe your use of social media?

If you're taught properly to use social media tools, you know that it's important to use your personal voice, and not just be promoting yourself all the time. Be a human being. Promote other people and other things, not just yourself.

And MailChimp, how did you settle on that particular site?

My boyfriend is a technologist, and he recommended that I set up a mailing list on MailChimp (rather than using regular email) because of all the tools it has to help you to better manage your mailing list. I don't have a huge mailing list at the moment—I'm still developing it—but I know if you have a huge mailing list, that it's far easier to use this system.

I know of a woman who's got 2,000 contacts on her mailing list. She sends out batches of eighty regular emails at a time until she gets them all out. It takes her hours to do it. Managing my list through MailChimp makes everything easy.

And what are some of the ancillary tools of MailChimp?

I can see who reads my e-letter and who doesn't. I can tell if curators or other important people read it, and I can see if it doesn't get through. I can get statistics on what parts of my newsletter people are clicking on—what people are interested in. And it tells me how many people have opened my newsletter or not opened it, and if people have unsubscribed.

Does it track when you send it and to whom?

Yes. It tracks everything for me.

And it provides templates for your communications?

Yes. You can use any one of their different templates to format your newsletter, and you can change it easily as well. It's almost like writing a blog post—it's that kind of interface. You can check drafts as you work, and you can schedule your e-letters to go out when you want, as well. That's what I do. I draft it, and then I get someone to proofread it. Then I send myself a test-email, so that I can see what it's actually going to look like. It also sends me a confirmation message once my newsletter's gone out, that tells me it has been sent and to how many people.

Does MailChimp provide you with good learning tools?

There's lots of how-to information on MailChimp. They have lots of tutorials and F-A-Qs.

Is there marketing advice as well as advice about how to use the site?

Yes. There's advice about how to build your mailing list and how to get more people to join it, and about how to get people to open and read your communications. That's a good thing about using these sites: There's lots of information about using Twitter, or Facebook and MailChimp on the sites. It takes a time investment to use social media; you have to maintain your presence and engage people.

Are you on Etsy.com as well?

I'm on Etsy, yes. That's how I sell my work online. I haven't had huge success on Etsy because I don't maintain a strong presence on it. I'm not producing a large amount of work that I can post all the time. But being on it has led to people buying work from me in person, after they've seen my work online.

So your principle source of generating direct sales is using social media?

Yes. Using social media to share my work brought attention to my altered books. As soon as I would finish one, I'd photograph it and upload it to Flickr, Twitter and my blog. The response from people was strong and immediate; there were inquiries about purchasing the work before I was ready to sell it. When I finally had a small show of the altered books, half of them were pre-sold because of my digital connections.

So instead of paying commissions, you have to make the time investment that you mention and maintain a constant presence, in order to be effective using social media.

Exactly. It's a lot of work, but it *does* work! I have yet to figure out how to make more money doing this. I'm not earning enough to live on, so that's the next piece of the puzzle for me. It may mean getting a part-time job. I'm okay with working part-time to support myself while I am making art. Right now, my partner helps support me. He understands what I'm trying to do because he's an entrepreneur and he encourages me. He appreciates the need to follow your passions, even if it's not always a money-making venture in the beginning. I am working on a five-year plan in order to be clear about what I want to do in the long-term, and to have goals to work towards.

I've done all kinds of random work over the years, but until I took the time to concentrate fully on my artistic career, I hadn't experienced much success. Since I came to Vancouver, I've exhibited regularly and sold more work, but to really be effective, I need to make a plan. I've shown work in a high number of shows this year and realize, in retrospect, that I will not repeat many of those initiatives in the future. I want to move beyond showing in cafes and theatre lobbies. I'm even becoming selective about which juried or group shows I want to participate in.

INTERVIEW: KRISTINE USES CONSTANT CONTACT

Do you remember when you first got started in creating artwork?

I dabbled in art as a kid, but I didn't really get into painting until about 1990, when I got interested in watercolours. I didn't like art in school.

You didn't?

I didn't like the teachers. I grew up in the Cowichan Valley (BC) and attended a small school. It's much better now, but in my day, all they cared about was that girls knew how to type, nurse, or teach.

And which one did you do?

I ended up becoming a bookkeeper. And I took typing.

And what brought you back to art?

I was living in Victoria at the time and working with several theatre companies, painting sets and crewing backstage. I loved working with like-minded people, but then my husband and I moved to Shawnigan Lake, and so I had to give that up. I was feeling the absence of creativity in my life when I walked into a frame shop in Mill Bay one day, and I saw some work by an artist named Carol Evans. I just about died when I saw it. I didn't realize that you could do that type of work—a kind of photorealism—in watercolour! I'd only seen watercolours in a style that wasn't for me, but when I saw her work, I thought, 'I am going to do that.' So I went out and bought watercolours and brushes and got my first Arches paper, and I entered heaven! Now I know that watercolour is the hardest medium to start with, but because I was painting in my kitchen, I didn't want turpentine and oil smells in my house, and watercolour is so easy to clean up.

And were you selling work?

Yes. I actually sold the very first serious watercolour painting I did. I used a whole sheet of Arches paper to do a big painting of two sandals on the dock at Mason's Beach. The people who owned Mason's Store saw it, liked it and bought it for a very good price.

How did your practice develop from there?

I did several more paintings of objects, very close up. I did one of sunglasses on the government railing, and I did one of a yellow Helly Hansen boot lying on a coil of rope on a dock. Then I published all three as limited edition prints through Manning Press in Sidney. I was just painting for the joy of it, but I did enter several of the Cowichan Valley Arts Council's annual exhibits, as well as other shows—I even won an Award of Merit and Award of Excellence.

And you were selling everything you did?

Yes, pretty much. And then I went to the Sooke Fine Arts Show and saw several large acrylics by Jimmy Wright. I decided to take his class in acrylics, mostly about using his dry brush technique. I loved the texture, and I loved that you could paint with greater freedom with acrylic paint. Watercolour was just too stressful for me; there was no room for error, and you had to do so much pre-planning so that you didn't lose the white space. I thought acrylics would let me be a lot more expressive and more relaxed in my painting.

After my husband and I divorced, I set up a small studio for myself. Having a studio meant I could leave everything set up and really focus on learning and practicing painting. I loved painting on canvas so much more than paper and, once they came out with wrapped canvas, I would paint the edges so that my work didn't need to be framed.

What was the next step?

I just kept painting in acrylic and entering shows. A group of friends and I did a show called *This Show's For Ewe* every year for ten years at Cowichan Bay Farm. We used the barns that were hung with proper gallery lighting and everything, and most of the work would sell. We would each mail out invitations to our own mailing lists, put up posters and advertise in the local papers, but I'd have to say that the show's growth in popularity was primarily due to word of mouth. Then I developed my first website.

And you were still doing accounting?

Yes, but part time, not full time. I had several businesses I was looking after.

Are you still doing both?

No. I'm mostly painting. I live on Cowichan Bay Farm now, and I've helped them a little bit with their bookkeeping, and I also have a friend who owns a gallery in Victoria whom I've been helping with accounting as well. Understanding accounting has enabled me to look after my own financial affairs, and when art sales are low, I just pick up some accounting work.

You seem to have a very pragmatic approach to working.

I have always considered working as an artist the same as operating any other small business. I know of artists who get upset because a gallery wants 50% commission. They don't see the value they get. But I had my own gallery, and so I know how much it costs to run one. Believe me, at the end of each year, my expenses were at least 50% of my income, and I was doing all my own marketing and promotion! So I tell my artist friends, I'm quite happy to give any gallery 50% because they handle it all. If you're going to be in business, you have to delegate. It's difficult being an artist and trying to do everything.

You operated your own gallery?

I started dating a fellow who was a furniture maker. He made beautifully crafted, very high-end wood furniture. I helped him with his business plan and start-up financing. We both agreed he needed a showroom, but because there is very little room for mark up on handcrafted solid wood furniture, he couldn't afford to pay the commission to anyone else who might sell it. So I proposed that we share a showroom.

I used to refer to the gallery as "a place to hang with artists, not just hang art" because I actually worked on site, as did another painter who came on board. People loved to watch us work, and to talk to us about what we were doing. For them, it was a much richer experience than just walking in and looking at work hanging there. I'm not talking about major collectors; I am largely talking about American tourists. They just loved our space. They would walk in with their little gold cards and walk away with three paintings, and they didn't have any problem with shipping. It was just great. The only reason the gallery closed after three years is that the fellow and I split up.

But the thing is, because I'd had this place in Victoria, other galleries took me on. They imagined that if I could sell enough work to support my own gallery, then they could sell my work to their customers. But I'm not prolific. A lot of artists will have a solo show, and they'll do twenty or thirty pieces. Well, I can't do that. I also can't afford to hang on to my paintings in order to create "a body of work." I have no income if I am not selling. I'm on my own; I don't have a partner to support me while I'm creating so everything I paint, I have to sell right away.

When I do paint for a group show, I will sometimes sell a piece before it can be delivered to the gallery. Some galleries don't like it if you sell work that's intended for their show. It's a very tricky business when you're representing yourself, and you have so many galleries selling your work as well.

Many galleries are distrustful and often rightfully so. They worry that people from their mailing list are contacting you directly and that you're selling behind their backs. But I would *never* do that. Anytime I've been approached directly by a known client of one of the galleries I'm with, I have said no and then told the gallery. But I think, when you have your own website and when you are selling your own work, it's hard to expect a gallery to take you on.

The thing is, I *do* have a mailing list, and I *do* have a following of my own. I have spent a lot of time developing a relationship with past clients who came into my gallery over those three years, so I'm not about to steer them to a gallery and then pay that gallery 50% for selling to a client who has always been mine. I had a woman contact me recently, and she bought eight pieces. She said that she'd been following my work for fifteen years, but she'd never been able to afford it until now. Now she had the money to buy it *and* the house to put it in.

And you use Constant Contact to manage your list?

One of the people who worked on my website, Carolynne Yardley, sent me a newsletter. She's up on all this social media stuff, and she knows about a lot of free things. She told me about Constant Contact and said I should try it, so I checked it out. I'm pretty good at stumbling my way through things, so I just started working with it. It's free up to a certain point, but I have a huge image gallery and a large mailing list, so I pay $15 a month.

How do you use it?

I plugged in all the names on my mailing list. At the time, I had two websites: One for my art and one for another project called Big Beautifuls®, a series of paintings of very large women, so I input separate mailing lists. One is strictly for people who are interested in Big Beautifuls®, and the other is my general mailing list. I also have a separate media list. I can send certain things out only to my Big Beautifuls® list, but I can also send news about my artwork to everybody. My media list gets everything I send out about shows.

I love that Constant Contact newsletters can include live links so that readers can just click to get directly to my website and my blog. And I always feature other artists and other shows, with links to their information.

And they provide templates for you to choose from for your communications?

Oh, yes! I find it's just so easy! And I appreciate the statistics you get. You can see what part of your newsletter interests people and who's reading it. You are told who chooses to opt off your list, and you get notice about addresses that are no longer active so that you can keep your list up to date. Plus, they have a "forward to a friend" feature at the bottom of your newsletter, and you can see if it's been forwarded, by whom and to how many people.

Some people just use email or an MS Word document to communicate. Why do you prefer using Constant Contact?

It's so much more professional looking than using regular email. I just love the look of it. I can upload my images easily into their templates, and I like the consistent look it gives to my communications.

For years I've been telling artists, okay, you're going to have a show, so now you've got to spend money on your business. I tell them that nobody's going to come and spend $2,000 on one of their paintings if they put a Xeroxed lime green flyer on car windshields at Thrifty's. That's just not going to happen. If, however, you spend the money and you get a proper full-colour invitation that's nicely designed, you'll have a lot more people coming to your show. And they'll bring friends. Using Constant Contact is the same thing. It's all about appearance, like the story of the Emperor's New Clothes. If you look like you're already successful, then everybody wants your work.

EPILOGUE

What Kristine says about the challenge of balancing personal sales with gallery sales is something all artists with market experience and who seek representation should consider. And Rachael's tips about how to be effective using social media echo the advice of many artists actively using them.

Web-based services, such as those offered on MailChimp and Constant Contact, are a Godsend for artists lacking in computer, graphic, sales and communication experience and training. They are communities that emulate the experience of this book: They offer you the opportunity to learn from the collective experience of other users of the site. Their instructional and peer-to-peer services augment the delivery and data-management service that is their core purpose.

As more and more people join these sites, they improve; the collective intelligence grows. They are, however, merely tools. How you use them will determine your success. In particular, how you write is crucial, so read the instructional materials the sites provide carefully, especially any information offered about sales copywriting. Be patient. Take in what you learn and consider it before you rush to send something out. Do as Rachael does: Send drafts to a few close friends for proofing before you circulate your communications widely. Do your research. Sign up to receive the e-newsletters of other artists to see how they use the medium, and good luck!

POSTSCRIPT

Not long after completing the interview, Rachael sent information about two other online resources that she uses and thought might be of interest to other artists. They are:

- **Cargoh**: www.cargoh.com
  Cargoh is a place where creative people can be seen, heard, and interconnect in one community driven marketplace.
- **Harvest**: www.getharvest.com
  Harvest is a business program that lets you track time in one integrated online application. It allows you to create online invoices and easily bill your clients and get paid faster by collecting online payments from your customers securely via the web.

LINKS

Constant Contact http://search.constantcontact.com
Fickr: www.flickr.com
MailChimp http://www.mailchimp.com
Sooke Fine Arts Show: /www.sookefinearts.com
Textile Museum of Canada: www.textilemuseum.ca

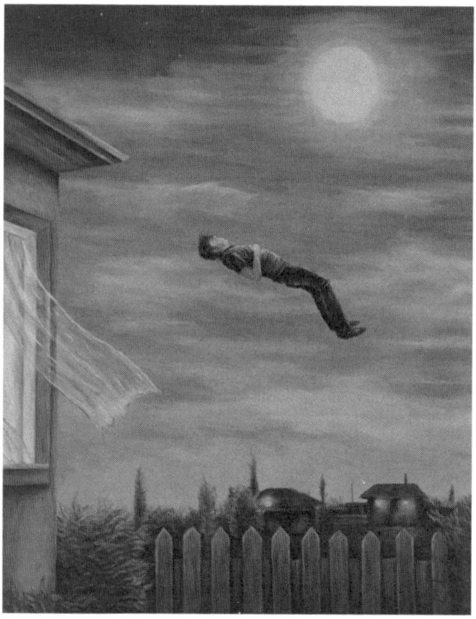

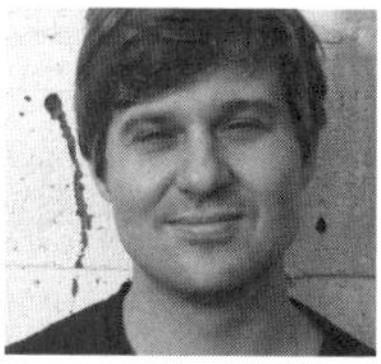

JUDE GRIEBEL, 1978

Leaving through windows; oil on canvas
2009; 60" x 48"
Courtesy of the Colart Canadian Art Collection

http://www.judegriebel.com

5 Jude Griebel

Residencies: Jude makes effective use of artist-in-residence programs to advance his career.

Date of interview: June 3, 2010

"After being in art school, you realize how important it is to be surrounded with peers, and to have access to people to talk with about your work—and to look at other artists producing work. You miss the feedback and energy when you maintain a private studio and work in isolation all day. Residencies offer a rich alternative to that."

— *Jude Griebel*

PROLOGUE

Jude is an emerging professional fine artist. He has built his career by spending considerable time in the studio and exhibiting, but it is his use of residency programs as a professional development tool that made me want to interview him.

Jude is a very personable young man with an intense earnestness about making art. His youthful enthusiasm was refreshing and infectious. He has been living "in the real world," as he calls it, for a few post-graduation years, and there is an increasing pragmatism when he talks about art as a career.

Being an "artist in residence" is a valuable learning and career advancement opportunity. Nothing beats experiential learning as a pedagogical methodology, and experiential learning is what residencies are about. The concept of "residency" is cousin to the concepts of "practicum" and "apprenticeship." Residencies can involve both mentoring and teaching, thereby putting the artist in the fulcrum of the student/master axis.

My own residency experiences have been some of the highlights of my career. My first was at the Banff Centre, where a scholarship earned me a three-week residency that inspired my commitment to a professional career in the arts. Later, in the U.S., a scholarship enabled me to participate in a conference of theatre artistic directors in residence. Both experiences gave me a vast amount of insight, creative energy, self confidence and contacts!

The friendships I made with other artists during my residencies lasted for decades, and some continue to motivate and inspire me today. Meeting Jude—so young, so earnest and so cleverly strategic at the beginning of his career—reminded me of the tremendous value of artist residencies.

I interviewed Jude in a café on Vancouver's Granville Island.

INTERVIEW

What do you think made the visual arts attractive to you?

My mother was an art conservator, so I was part of a strong art community. I had the opportunity to visit a lot of people's studios with her, and I made friends of many artists in Canada and abroad.

I spent most of my time drawing. I taught myself to draw, copying the illustrations in my father's medical books, and I spent a lot of time in my mother's studio because often she didn't have a babysitter. After high school, I realized that I wanted to have a career in the visual arts, so I went to Emily Carr University and began my art education. I took fine arts with a focus on printmaking, and during my schooling, I won a student scholarship with Malaspina Printmakers (a Vancouver-based printmakers collective with a large studio and gallery).

What attracted you to printmaking?

I think printmaking was the right platform to launch my career because multiples are easy to exhibit in other cities. The great thing about printmaking, is that gives you an instant community all over the world. Print shops and studios gather community around them, and then they form relationships with other print studios so that they can exchange artists and exhibitions. As a printmaker, you inherit links to places all over the world. Also, I was able to sell work out of Malaspina, and through them I was able to participate in some international exhibitions and residencies. They also host a great Artists-in-Residence program, so I was able to meet all these wonderful people from Spain and Japan who were guest artists.

What happened after you graduated?

When I left Emily Carr, I kind of eased into Malaspina. They provided access to their studio and facilities, and gave me a community of artists with whom to work on a professional level. Their resources allowed me to maintain the same production level with my work as I had enjoyed while a student at Emily Carr. When you're in art school, you have nothing but time to create work, but when you leave art school, you're faced with the reality of supporting yourself. Consequently, time in the studio becomes an incredible luxury.

I took some part time jobs, and I worked at Malaspina to offset my studio costs and to pay for my studio rent and materials. I also worked with Peter Braune at New Leaf Editions. With him, and in collaboration with a lot of his talented and established artist/clients, I could talk about their process as I helped to make editions of their prints.

Then I found gallery representation in Vancouver with the Elissa Cristall Gallery and then at Bau-Xi Gallery, where I had my first solo exhibition of paintings in 2005. But then I left Vancouver. I wanted a change of scene and chose Montreal because of its proximity to New York where I've been spending some time. Also, in Vancouver I couldn't find desirable studio space at an affordable price.

What made you change to painting from printmaking?

I became more interested in exploring and developing imagery more quickly than I could with printmaking. And with painting, I was able to work on a much larger scale. Also, I find that there isn't a huge awareness of work on paper in Canada, compared to other places. Printmaking here, though it seems to be making a resurgence, has been considered a more archival medium. The work isn't often viewed in a critical context. I wanted to exhibit in public galleries and artist-run centres, and printmaking, as a medium, seems to be relegated to other printmaking centres. I felt very limited by that.

And themes emerged as you started painting?

I began at Emily Carr intent on becoming a children's book illustrator. I began illustrating some books and realized that I was not necessarily interested in making images for children to understand. I was more interested in explaining things to myself, using symbols and images compiled through my own experience with children's books. I took a number of characters from children's books and constructed costumes based on the characters, but I modeled them on peers from my adult life. This became the basis for my first comprehensive body of print work and paintings.

What attracted you to the various Artist-in-Residence programs that have become such a large part of your career?

After being in art school, you realize how important it is to be surrounded with peers, and to have access to people to talk with about your work—and to look at other artists producing work. You miss the feedback and energy when you maintain a private studio and work in isolation all day. Residencies offer a rich alternative to that.

Being surrounded by people discussing painting on a regular basis is wonderful. I was at the Vermont Studio Centre in 2009. It is quite a significant residency; there were fifty artists working there when I was there. The centre had taken over a small town called Johnson, Vermont, as a campus, and there was a schedule of guest critics who came in—two per week, mostly from New York City. They would do individual studio visits with whoever signed up for them. My residencies have been an important source of critical feedback.

Is there a typical experience to your residencies?

There are many levels of residencies. Each one is very different. Some of them are funded through the Canada Council or other supporting agencies; for others, their funding coming from private patrons or from fees the artists pay. For many residencies, you have to pay room and board and sometimes a studio fee. This is because the host agency expects you to secure grant funding. However, due to the competitive nature of grants, there is a high probability you will wind up paying out of your own pocket.

Some places that I've visited have asked me to leave a piece of work behind for their collection. I think that is fair exchange for being somewhere and being hosted. Many residencies offer the opportunity to give artist talks and workshops; they are often paid sessions to help the artist earn money to offset costs. Also, I've received travel grants that enabled me to experience numerous international residencies.

The first residency I did was at St. Michaels Printshop in St. John's, Newfoundland. It is one of the oldest printmaking studios in Canada. They paid for my airfare and paid me an artist's fee, and I believe they even gave me a living stipend. It was very well funded. I applied for it, was accepted, and got my first travel grant to get there and produce prints during a summer. I think I was able to get it so early in my career because I was active in the printmaking community, plus I'd had the experience of working at Malaspina.

Do you have some favourite residencies?

Japan was a wonderful experience. I went to a printmaking studio in Shin-Yokohama with two other members of Malaspina Printmakers. We went there for the opening of an international printmaking exhibition that was a collaborative effort between Malaspina, the print studio in Japan, and a print studio in the Netherlands. We were there at the same time as Dutch artists and we were all working in the studio at the same time. There was incredible support from the Japanese artists; we were taken out everywhere. We had beautiful dinners every night, plus there were several exhibition openings to attend.

The other memorable residency would be the one through the Klondike Institute of Art and Culture. The Yukon and Dawson City are such amazing sites. The history of the gold rush still exists in the frontier-town buildings, so you almost feel like you're living in a museum when you're there. I went there because I had been making some paintings, exploring the metaphor of ghosts. Someone told me about the residency program there, and that it was in a historic house where several artists-in-residence had witnessed supernatural experiences. I was interested in the idea of a historic house in which artists had lived, produced work and had these experiences.

I got a project grant to interview past artists and residents who had stayed in the house, and recorded their stories about staying and producing work there. Then I created paintings based on their stories, inside the actual space. At the same time, I researched the history of the house in the local archives and put it together as a book project. I received a Canada Council Project Grant to fly there, do the work and self-publish a book based on the experience. Because my work is very self-reflective, it's not very often I do a project that's based on the experience of others. This project was the first opportunity I had to really bridge my own interests with a community and historical narrative. I was there for two months.

Do you need to be good at writing proposals to secure a residency?

Yes, you do. Writing and submitting applications has become a regular exercise for me. I've received a lot of rejections, but I have a rule: Keep at least ten proposals "out there." When an answer comes in, I send another application off. It's something I routinely do. I like writing about my work and getting talented people to critique it.

Did you take specific training in proposal writing?

I took a course in professional practice in art school, but I think that's one aspect of my practice that I had to develop on my own. You must be able to explain how your work applies to the purposes of the residency. Centres and galleries get many proposals; you have to provide a specific and interesting reason that matches their objectives.

Is living exclusively on sales and through residencies going okay?

I would say so, I mean I eat well, I have a studio I like. I would like to be more comfortable, sure, but I think most artists would. It's the past few years that have been very hard due to the economy. Sales are down. I've really felt it in the last couple of years, but I'm hoping things will get better. Still, I wake up excited to work every day, and I have a lot I'm working on right now. I'm traveling to Iceland soon, to an art institute called the Nes Residency; I have an exhibition opening there in a town called Skagaströnd, and a while after that, I'm returning to Iceland for an exhibition of ten years of my work on paper at Ílsensk Grafík in Reykjavik. Plus, I'm starting my grad studies soon at the school at the Art Institute of Chicago.

How have you learned about your residencies?

I learned about my first residencies through the printmaking community and artist-run centres. I learned about others through artists I met at residencies. There are also good online resources for residencies, including the Res Artis site and Trans Artists, among others. These sites can be especially helpful when matching the resources and scope of a centre to your project. (Contact information is listed at the end of this chapter.)

Is there something valuable about the application process that you might want to share with other artists considering a residency?

I think it is important to understand what you are looking for from the experience, and be able to communicate your idea in your writing. Why do you feel that your project should be undertaken in a certain geographical context? How will it benefit both your experience (in creating the work) and the community in which you are making it?

Although residencies can be very much about focus and isolation, there is always an element of exchange present. Many residencies have programs that have themes or are media specific, so it's important to find the right fit. Research can require a lot of time but will result in a convincing proposal and allow you to secure funding through grants.

JUDE'S RESIDENCIES

2011 *Artist Residency*, CHHAAP Baroda Workshop, Gujarat, India
2010 *Artist Residency*, Nes Center, Iceland
2009 *Self-Directed Residency*, Banff Centre for the Arts, Canada
Artist Grant and Residency, The Vermont Studio Center, USA
2007 *Artist Residency*, Frans Masereel Centrum, Belgium
Artist Residency, Klondike Institute of Art and Culture, Canada
Artist Residency, Atelier Imago, Moncton, Canada
2005 *Artist Residency*, Workshop OM, Shin-Yokohama, Japan
2003 *Artist Residency*, St. Michael's Printshop, St. John's, Canada

EPILOGUE

I was impressed with the wisdom of Jude's decisions to work with mentoring agencies such as Malaspina Printmakers and New Leaf Editions. These apprenticeships brought Jude into contact with accomplished artists. Also, although Jude first found himself drawn to printmaking, he knew that his career ambitions required that he master painting. He was wise to move to painting, but he was equally astute to keep making multiples to sell (at a lower price point).

Jude has used residencies strategically. They have enabled him to produce work and live in environments that stimulate his imagination and provide him with unique resources. As well, the contacts he has made while in residency programs have provided him with valuable peer relationships and furthered international awareness of his work.

This young man is single and without dependents. For him, the demanding lifestyle of an emerging artist undertaking numerable residencies is not a challenge; the benefits far outweigh any disadvantages. However, the artist leading a busy and hectic life, deeply rooted in her or his community, can also benefit from the ideal creative oasis that a residency offers. And for established artists, a residency can serve as a powerful source of renewal and site-specific inspiration, providing benefits that endure for the rest of a career.

Residencies can work for every artist, stimulating and/or reviving a career or a body of work.

RESEARCHING RESIDENCY RESOURCES:

Google provides a lot of information about local and international residency opportunities available to visual artists. The residencies that came up in my searches cover a vast range of media, length of tenure, eligibility, cost, subsidy availability, and responsibilities. You have no option but to spend some time online researching them in order to find the one that best suits your needs. Use Google thoughtfully, choosing key words such as "international" and/or "academic," plus "visual arts residencies;" or "visual art residencies in [your medium or a specific county]."

The more ideal the residency sounds, the more likely you will have a lot of competition if you apply. To compete for a highly desirable residency will require (in addition to a meritorious artistic mission) excellent references, skillful writing and professional experience.

The Canada Council website has a list of the international residency opportunities that it supports through a peer adjudicated process. The Artists in Canada website lists international residency opportunities, and the Banff Centre hosts the *Leighton Artists' Colony* residency program for artists of various disciplines including the visual arts,. Their adjudicated application process is explained on their website. (A link to all these resources is provided at the end of this chapter.)

Res Artis is the largest existing online network of artist residency programs. It represents the interests of more than three hundred centres and organizations in fifty countries that offer international artists facilities and conditions conducive for making art.

Trans Artists is a knowledge centre site focused on Artist-in-Residence opportunities. On it, you can find all about international Artist-in-Residence programs as well as opportunities for artists to stay and work abroad.

The best information about residencies may come from fellow artists in your community or artists you find through research on the Internet. I have often posed questions to artists I do not know, but whose website has revealed experience of interest, to great success. The Skype Internet telephone service has also allowed me to have free and visually rich conversations with artists whom I have never met in person, but whose experience has educated me even though they live in other cities or countries.

TIPS ON APPLYING FOR A RESIDENCY

An inherent part of residencies is their divergence in form and nature. Each application process is different; host agencies review applications in the context of their specific eligibility criteria and applicant experience. As a professional artist, you must develop cohesive and compelling artist's statements to unite your bodies of work. An application for a residency needs a succinct and intriguing statement of intent to be successful—as eloquent and thoughtful a statement as you apply to your artwork.

Provide impressive references. I have been a collector of letters of reference throughout my career; I support any application I make with carefully selected professional references to increase my chances of success. Obviously, the more respected and known your references, the better for your proposal. Academic or other professional references are very powerful.

When you apply, read the criteria for eligibility and the objectives of the program carefully and mirror back your clear understanding of their aims in your proposal. Address every one of their objectives directly and have peers or mentors assess your application against the eligibility criteria before you submit it.

CREATING YOUR OWN "RESIDENCY"

I have often created my own "residency" experience. As a young man, I quit a good job teaching at a secondary school in order to spend the ensuing year collecting Employment Insurance while apprenticing at Vancouver's Arts Club Theatre. My E.I. caseworker approved of the re-training strategy because the theatre agreed to employ me at the end of the practicum. For a year, I worked in a self-directed training program that taught me all the skills I required for a career in the arts that lasted my lifetime.

As a writer, I have twice created my own "residencies" in order to escape into the cocoon-like creative environment they afford, free from the demands of my home and workplace. When an important deadline is looming, or a particularly difficult project requires long periods of intense concentration, I book a room with a kitchen in a motel in Palm Springs, that has a swimming pool and a restaurant. I stay for one or two weeks and I never leave the grounds. Each stay has been highly productive and although unsubsidized, entirely free of any obligations other those that are self-determined.

For an uplifting experience designed to stimulate and educate me, I went to Florence, Italy for a three-week "residency" of my own design. I rented a suite with a kitchen in a central place (Palazzo Ricasoli), and bought myself several hours of services from a local guide with a PhD in Renaissance Florentine art. I had written an essay about my objectives for my stay that I gave to her, asking that she take me on an annotated journey through the architecture and art of the city and its museums that served my objectives. I also rented the studio of a local artist wherein I, and the artist/friends who were with me, could create work stimulated by sketches done during the annotated tours of the guide.

LINKS

Artists in Canada: artistsincanada.com/php/~studio.php
Banff Centre: www.banffcentre.ca
Bau-Xi Gallery: www.bau-xi.com
Canada Council: www.canadacouncil.ca
Elissa Cristall Gallery: www.cristallgallery.com
Ílsensk Grafík: www.islenskgrafik.is
Klondike Institute of Art and Culture: http://www.kiac.org
Malaspina Printmakers: www.malaspinaprintmakers.com
New Leaf Editions: www.newleafeditions.com
Nes Artist Residency: http://neslist.is
Palazzo Ricasoli: http://www.ricasoli.net
Res Artis: www.resartis.org
Skype: www.skype.com
Trans Artists: www.transartists.org

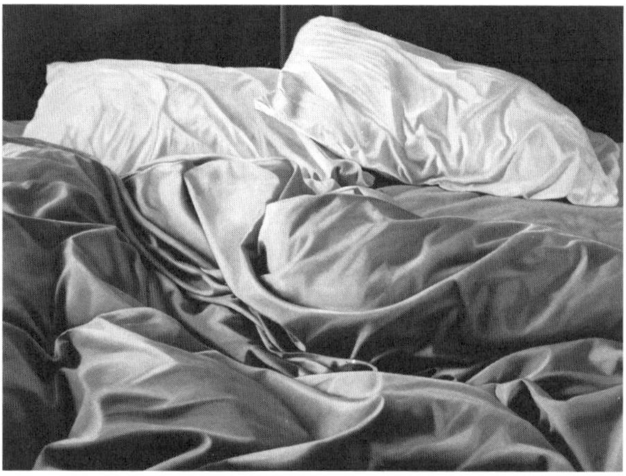

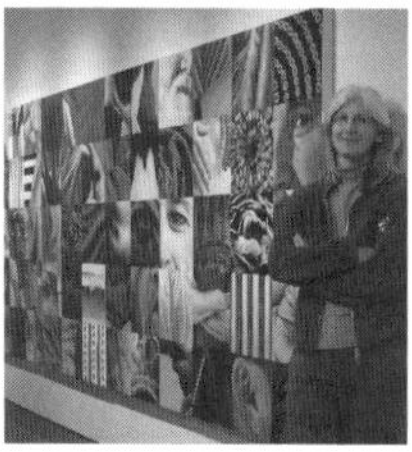

MADELEINE WOOD, 1961

lorilol; oil on canvas
2008; 36"x48"

Madeleine in front of "So Much For Love"
oil on canvas; 2005; 60" by 18' x 5'

http://www.madeleinewood.com

6 Madeleine Wood

Risk: Madeleine took the risk that many artists consider and desire, but are afraid to undertake.

Date of interview: July 7, 2010

"Renting the studio was a pivotal decision for me. It was profoundly rewarding to have a clean white space in which to work, and it made me part of a community. It also led to thinking about taxation issues and about setting myself up as a business. Having the studio forced me to take myself seriously as an artist."

— *Madeleine Wood*

PROLOGUE

The most often expressed desire of my students is to earn a living working exclusively as a visual artist. This is the "artist's dream." Some young artists adopt the clichéd starving or subsistence lifestyle but a great many of artists who earn the entirety of their income from art making are subsidized financially by a life partner or their family.

The difficulty of earning all one's living from a creative practice often forces artists into some degree of employment and, over time, they find it harder and harder to risk giving up employment income in order to have the full-time creative career they want. Making the problem worse: Artists and art buyers thrive in dense urban cities that are expensive places to live and work. Many young and emerging artists have career objectives that include a desire to live comfortably in urban Canada; they have no idea how difficult it will be to fulfill their desire.

Madeleine decided to make "the dream" her reality. I first met her through the Alliance for Arts and Culture in Vancouver, which was running a government-funded employment program called *Self-employed Arts-related Contractors for Hire* (S.E.A.R.C.H.) that honed the skills of under-employed cultural workers. Madeleine was a staff member. I met her again, in a different context when I happened on her studio during Vancouver's East Side Culture Crawl. Not long after that meeting, I heard that Madeleine had quit her job in order to live exclusively as a painter.

Why did I choose to interview Madeleine over any number of other artists living full-time as an artist?

1. Because I admire Madeleine's work and technical skills. She produces highly professional work that is marketable and sincere.
2. It's not easy to find someone living exclusively from the proceeds of their practice; that is, who is not earning income from even modest ancillary jobs and/or being supported, in part, by a partner's income.
3. Also, because such a high percentage of artists who are successful at establishing a creative practice are male, I chose to interview Madeleine, whose success, therefore, is that much more impressive.

I interviewed Madeleine over the telephone while she was in her home studio in Fanny Bay on Vancouver Island.

INTERVIEW

Do you recall an early start to making art?

Art has always been in my life. It was my first language. According to my parents, I didn't speak until I was about four and a half. I remember drawing being 'my place,' my home. It was unselfconscious and I drew all the time, otherwise I was lost.

And you pursued that interest in school?

Oh yes! As I grew older and more conscious of the attention I was getting, everyone, including me, assumed I would become an artist. I have now come to believe that my visual acuity grew out of necessity. I was born with extremely poor eyesight; after eye surgery, I used drawing to overcome the weakness.

And you pursued training in the visual arts after high school?

Not right after. I spent a year working in Israel, then another at Bible School, and joined the militia before being accepted at Emily Carr University where I did first and second year. But I got pregnant, and didn't continue. Eight years later, in 1991, I returned and completed my diploma as a mature student. Then I got my Master of Fine Arts degree at Concordia University in Montreal. My studies gave me five consecutive years to build a strong painting practice.

At this time, were you working? Were you selling any work?

I supported myself and my daughter as a desktop publisher for six years. But after reaching my creative limit, I quit and took out student loans to return to school. Selling my paintings was incidental then, although I did sell some. It was more about being part of a community of artists and getting exhibition experience—that whole process of putting together a show from concept to installation is very satisfying. And defending my thesis exhibition was a fulfilling way to end my graduate studies.

What happened next?

I went about re-integrating into the Vancouver community. Taking the S.E.A.R.C.H. program was one of the first steps that reinforced my desire to be a professional artist. I was then able to find contract work related to my field: I was a Vancouver Art Gallery animateur for three shows, taught studio classes for various schools, took staff positions at Emily Carr, and then I got a full-time arts administration job at the Alliance for Arts and Culture. Over five years, I was gradually able to decrease my working hours at the Alliance and increase my hours in the studio.

After my daughter became independent, I took further risks. In 2003, I moved into co-op housing, quit my job, stopped driving and started living more frugally. All this enabled me to paint full-time. I had set up my space in William Clark Studios and I knew it was important to develop a balanced routine, so I started to treat working in my studio like a job. I'd wake up in the morning and do administrative stuff on my computer when I felt mentally sharp, and then I would get down to the studio, ten minutes away, and work hard for the rest of the day. Then I'd find balance by drumming in the evenings.

Renting the studio was a pivotal decision for me. It was profoundly rewarding to have a clean white space in which to work, and it made me part of a community. It also led to thinking about taxation issues and about setting myself up as a business. Having the studio forced me to take myself seriously as an artist.

Since my studio was on the East Side of Vancouver, I was able to be part of the Eastside Culture Crawl. The Crawl was a perfect springboard for my career; it gave me a deadline and a focus. I did small paintings to appeal to a certain market, and sold quite a few. Also, I met lots of people—about a thousand people would go through my studio in a weekend. It was gratifying to develop relationships and make direct sales of my own!

How did you start building sales?

I continued participating in the Crawl every year, and then Ian Tan approached me about exhibiting in his gallery. I gained valuable experience there, in a very short time, producing four solo shows and selling a lot of paintings. Five years ago, he moved to a new space on Granville Street where I still exhibit. Ian helped me feel like a partner right from the beginning of our relationship. In the artist-gallery relationship, it's vital that you work together and build trust.

And you knew the ian tan gallery would be only one part of the puzzle?

For me, there are two forms of recognition: Money and critical feedback. It didn't take long for me to realize that I would need a number of galleries. After a long journey exploring various cities, I'm pleased to be represented by four galleries (ian tan gallery, Madrona Gallery, Nanaimo Art Gallery and Terence Robert Gallery) as well as by a showroom in Wisconsin. By expanding my markets, I hope to increase my sales.

And then there are the public galleries. They are important because they give me an opportunity to develop ideas that reflect something closer to my heart and that are often too intimate or provocative for a commercial setting. I will always have public shows as a contemporary artist. Public shows don't usually generate sales, but they do offer artist fees and media coverage. Fortunately, my work straddles both public and commercial contexts.

So, it's been seven years that you've been earning your living as an artist. Do you regret the decision you made to take on the artistic career full time?

Not for a minute! It's something that I'm proud of and feel is my true calling. There are, of course, times when it lacks luster. It can get that way if I have to produce a lot of work for too many shows, too close together. Painting can feel mechanical and repetitive under pressure, but being practical, I know that if I keep painting—because I do have a good sense of composition and colour—that people will like what I do.

Like most artists, I worry about money. But now, instead of stewing, I get to work, demonstrating to myself as much as to others, how important art making is to me.

Part of your transition involved moving to a less expensive place to live. How has it been, being so removed from the city and the artistic community that meant so much to you?

Very worthwhile. Withdrawing from the urban environment this year has given me a higher quality of life that I only dreamt about in the past. In this naturally beautiful, quiet and clean place, I can live simply and produce more. I have a wonderful partner, and we own a house for the first time in my life. It's rustic—we're in the middle of renovating—but I'm looking out at half an acre of land and woods above a wildlife sanctuary with beaches all around. It's much nicer than working above Clark Drive. I miss Vancouver at times, and I communicate regularly with my daughter and friends. My computer has become very important, and I am joining new communities here on Vancouver Island.

If you had a roomful of people contemplating giving up their day jobs to go full-time into their art career, what would you tell them?

Don't expect too much too soon. Build your savings, your ideas, your art inventory, and put it out to market. Give it time, and be gracious. If it's important to you, you'll sustain it, and it will sustain you.

EPILOGUE

"Don't expect too much, too soon" is great advice. Madeleine grew into creative self-reliance. She was pragmatic, taking jobs when she needed to. She delayed the establishment of her full-time creative career until she could afford, financially and emotionally, to take the risk. Madeleine kept moving forward, taking incremental steps until she was ready to take a big leap and live a life of creative self-employment—the dream life that so many artists want but are afraid to try.

Her risk has been rewarded. She is earning enough to support her chosen lifestyle, and has, as a result of her work and experience, found enormous satisfaction from human, not material, response to her work.

TRANSITION PROGRAMS

If you are an artist with employment history, you may qualify for retraining assistance through federal or provincial government retraining programs. Use Google and the manpower sections of governments' websites to research possibilities such as these two operating in the Vancouver area.

1. SEEDS: The Self-Employment and Entrepreneur Development Society (SEEDS: www.seedsbdc.com) is a non-profit society dedicated to entrepreneur development and the growth of businesses. SEEDS has helped more than 1,800 individuals transition to self-employment.

The SEEDS program assists unemployed residents living in the Lower Mainland who are legally entitled to work in Canada—this includes artists quitting jobs to enter into self-employment, but you must have a strong business case for your creative enterprise and have an active EI claim (or be collecting EI) to be eligible. Also, you may be eligible for their General Self-Employment Program if you have:

- "reach back status" (have collected EI anytime during the past three years)
- collected maternity or parental benefits any time during the past five years
- a physical or mental impairment that restricts your ability to get or maintain long term employment.

If you qualify for the General Self-Employment Program, the Government of Canada may provide funding of $300 per week for 48 weeks, while you participate in the program.

2. THE LANGARA COLLEGE SELF-EMPLOYMENT PROGRAM

www.langara.bc.ca/management-business/self-employment

The Langara College Self-Employment Program is funded through the Canada-BC Labour Market Development Agreement and operated by Langara College in collaboration with the Entrepreneur Assistance Society of Metro Vancouver. The program is designed to assist people on Employment Insurance (EI), or those whose EI benefits have run out, to successfully start their own businesses. The program is delivered in two phases, and it allows participants to collect 48 weeks of income support from the federal and/or provincial governments while developing their business.

The program provides workshops and seminars on developing business plans and business management. Providing counseling and support services, the program helps build confidence and reduces the anxiety of starting a new business. Results from a 2008 program survey determined that 96% of past participants (who responded) were still in business, with combined annual sales of more than $3 million.

Another valuable resource for artists transitioning to full time employment is Canada's Cultural Human Resources Council.

CULTURAL HUMAN RESOURCES COUNCIL

The Cultural Human Resources Council (CHRC) brings together cultural workers and employers to address training, career development and other human resource issues. The CHRC works for, and with, all the cultural industries and arts disciplines including the visuals arts and crafts, film and digital media. CHRC also works on cross-sector issues such as cultural management, career management and export marketing.

The CHRC has always had an emphasis on self-employed artists. The self-employment rate in Canada 's cultural labour force, at 21% (2009), is almost three times higher than the rate in the overall labour force, at 8%. Among painters, sculptors and other visual artists, the number of self-employed is at 67%; among artisans and crafts persons, 50% are self-employed.

With these statistics in mind, CHRC has developed certain materials to assist the self-employed visual artist and crafts person. These are featured on their website:

- *The Art of Managing Your Career* includes discipline enhancements for visual artists and crafts people. (www.culturalhrc.ca/amyc/index-e.asp)
- *Export Marketing of Cultural Goods and Services* (www.culturalhrc.ca/em/index-e.asp)
- The site also has a link to *The Mind's Eye - Careers in Culture* a book for visual artists and crafts persons, complete with voice testimonials of practicing artists. (http://www.culturalhrc.ca/careersinculture/mindseye/e/index.asp).

LINKS

Alliance for Arts and Culture: www.allianceforarts.com
East Side Culture Crawl: www.eastsideculturecrawl.com
ian tan gallery: www.iantangallery.com
Madrona Gallery: www.madronagallery.com
Nanaimo Art Gallery: www.nanaimogallery.ca
Terence Robert Gallery: www.terencerobertgallery.com
William Clark Studios: via the East Side Culture Crawl website

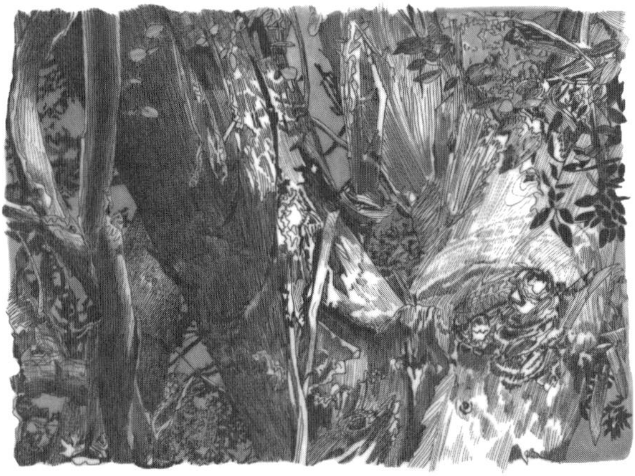

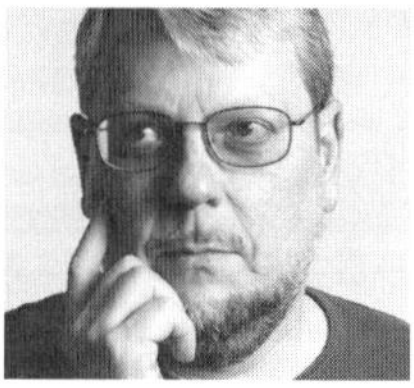

GARY SIM, 1951
Eucalyptus, Barclay Park.
Pen & ink with india ink brushpen on vellum
2006; 10" X 12"

http://www.sim-publishing.com

7 Gary Sim

Marketing: Gary very successfully sold a lot of art by organizing a unique auction.

Date of interview: July 3, 2010

"My auction was a "one-day" thing that worked really well.... I had 44 of my own images for sale, plus 76 works by 38 other artists from my collection.... Sixteen lots sold before the auction, 46 sold at the Salon (auction), and two were sold afterwards."

— *Gary Sim*

PROLOGUE

Many of my students are mature emerging artists who have enrolled in my class because they have recently retired and have an interest in the visual arts. Others of my students who still have jobs, frequently betray a desire to quit their job, in order to earn 100% of their income from a creative practice. I tell all of them (and everyone who seeks to transition to a creative career) that it is best to begin the transition years ahead of the date they choose to retire or quit their job.

I interviewed Gary because he is an artist with a demanding full-time job who has developed a very active and professional part-time visual art career in his home/studio. When Gary retires from his job with an architectural firm, he will have a healthy existing practice and large customer base to support him creatively and financially.

I met Gary through my work with the Alumni Association of Emily Carr University. I chose to put myself on his mailing list because I was impressed by his work and by the cleverness and professionalism of his marketing practices. Of particular interest to me was an initiative he took to organize an auction of his work and the work of some of his peers.

Whereas organising an auction my not be for you, doing one in partnership with other artists may be feasible. Or, if not an auction, taking another self-directed or collective initiative is a worthy lesson to draw from Gary's experience. Some self-determined exercise has been part of the career of a great many successful artists.

I met with Gary in his home/studio.

INTERVIEW

What is the job you have?

I work full-time for DGBK Architects. Their office is just a few blocks from my home/studio. I do construction administration for them—project management.

And for the long-term, does your job afford you a pension?

Architecture doesn't really offer pensions at this point. Some bigger companies have stock options but not the one I'm with, so it's Canada Pension, doing my own thing with RRSPs and selling art for my retirement.

And when did you first start getting involved with art?

I still have a grade one sketchbook with stick figures in crayons and jet planes in the sky. I did drafting in high school, and that got me into technical drawing. I did a lot of detailed pen-and-ink drawing in the sixties, and I did weaving, photography and even ceramics for a while.

When did you start to sell your work?

In 1969, when I was eighteen, I sold a pen and ink drawing to a friend for $300, and it was like "Oh that's neat," but it never really twigged that I could make money at drawing! I didn't sell anything else for another thirty years.

So later in life it came back to you?

Every few years I would draw something, but I never drew continuously. But I started drawing more, and then I got involved with the Alcuin Society in Vancouver—they produce the Antiquarian Book Fair at the Vancouver Public library, and they have a journal called *Amphora* that was doing a series of featured artists, so I emailed them. They were more interested in book illustrations and wanted wood engravings or linocut prints that could be "letter-pressed" into a limited edition book, so I started doing prints. They were fun to do, and I could do them easily in my home studio. I found a press that worked perfectly; it's like printing money, in a way.

How did you first start to sell your prints?

I had an epiphany when I asked myself, "Where am I going?" I realized that I was doing nothing to give back to society; I wasn't doing any volunteer work, making donations or doing public service—it was all me, me, me. So I started volunteering for groups such as Vancouver's Public Art Committee, Emily Carr Alumni Society and the Architectural Institute of BC (AIBC). As a result of getting involved with the AIBC, they gave me a place in a two-person show, and I sold sixteen pieces of the roughly twenty-five I had in the show. And I thought "Hey, that worked!" Which is kind of funny because the curator, Colin Wong, selected pieces that I wouldn't have chosen.

Have you been able to repeat that experience?

No, but I keep hoping to.

Well, that's one reason I wanted to interview you. Rather than waiting for a good sales opportunity to happen, you made sales happen with an auction.

You have to show your work; if people don't see it, they can't buy it. My auction was a "one-day" thing that worked really well. It was called The BC Arts Salon and it was a complex affair thrown together in three weeks. It helped to have already done a huge amount of work on my collection—I had maintained things like titling, labeling, pricing, taking illustrative images etcetera, and I had experience, having worked part-time for an auctioneer. Also, a friend who is an auctioneer volunteered to work for free.

I hired one of my friend's auction crew, plus three women I know, to handle any problems (one artist, one accountant, one office manager). They divvied up the work and handled all sales, shipping and credit card/debit transactions. The restaurant owner (La Gavroche, where I'm a regular) let me have the restaurant free for the day, and gave me fixed prices for crew meals, as well as breaks on the drinks and hors d'oeuvres for the customers. They also gave us the run of the place to rearrange tables and chairs, and to replace their art with mine. It was a deluxe venue that had to be restored for regular service by 5:00 p.m. After the auction, Jack Evrensel came by to say hello and, after asking about the success of the Salon, offered me free use of his restaurant, CinCin, for the same kind of event in the future!

There was lots of paperwork to do: I had to make bidder numbers, bidder forms and absentee bid forms, catalogues, invoices, artist biographies, lot number stickers, etc. Digital images had to be made for our catalogues and our Salon website , and a lot of marketing initiatives were undertaken. But I had 44 of my own images for sale (12 sold), plus 76 works by 38 other artists from my collection. I had a wide range of mediums in a wide range of presentations. Also, I had a collection of my pamphlets and greeting cards for sale. Asking prices ranged from $2.00 to $6,000.00; prices realized ranged from free to $3,000.00. Sixteen lots sold before the auction, 46 at the Salon, and two were sold afterwards.

Who did you invite?

Everyone I knew. I have about 200 people on my mailing list: Friends, people who have bought work or maybe who are interested in my work, collectors, friends of friends, everyone I could think of. Because it was a sale *and* auction, up until the auction started, you could buy the artwork at the reserve or list price. Thankfully, I sold $2,000 worth of work before the show opened, so I knew that my expenses were covered.

Many success stories involve some element of risk-taking.

It was risky in that I might have lost as much as $2,000 on expenses, but even if I had, I would have had great exposure and a good day of talking to people. However, I sold quite a bit of art in the end, and I've had some repeat business since. I'm hoping that I'll eventually have enough critical mass of followers or collectors to build the Art Salon into a regular thing. The problem has been that I am employed full-time, and I don't have the production level that a full-time artist has.

So, you're doing some writing related to the visual arts, some illustration work, you're selling work through traditional outlets, plus you've done innovative things like the auction. You strike me as being quite entrepreneurial.

You have to be creative about finding places to put your art—places to connect with potential buyers. For example, the restaurant where I had the auction has three permanent pieces up now, and I had a sale because of that exposure recently.

Do you pay the restaurant a commission?

I've offered a commission, but he refused to take it. He said he was doing a favour for a friend. He likes the art, and so do his customers. He has other artists up as well; it's a form of patronage, really. He's got very cosmopolitan clientele so it's a great place to show work. He doesn't like to have price tags on the wall or anything, but he'll happily sell work or put me in touch with interested people. I think it's great to find a place like that and a man like him.

What other sales outlets have been successful for you?

I've sold a number of prints at Malaspina Printmakers. I've sold 10 to 12 prints through their print racks and exhibitions. I'm also an active member of the Federation of Canadian Artists (FCA) and I sell through their gallery as well. The FCA is an amazing organization for people who fit comfortably into their mandate. I've had my work published in their magazine, *Art Avenue*, and they've used one of my drawings as a background image on their e-newsletter. I post my work on my FCA member page on their website.

Do you do any cards?

Yes. I have them out when I'm doing a show, and I've got them listed on my website.

Can people buy off your website?

I don't have an e-store set up but I welcome email orders.

Do people who see your work online contact you to buy?

That, basically, doesn't happen. My website gets a lot of hits, but nobody buys through it. It's the least useful source of sales I have... I get a lot of hits; 45 people a day look at my website, but I get no sales.

You participated in a co-operative "fair" at Heritage Hall (Vancouver). How was that experience?

That was the Mid-Main Art Fair that Edna Bardell organized. She booked the hall and invited several artists she knew to take part. We were sixteen artists in all.

And how did you do?

I sold one original pen and ink drawing from a series of non-representational drawings. And then I sold somewhere between 60 to 80 cards. It was two dollars a card, so I was practically giving them away, but they cost me only 60 cents to print. I laser print them here and bag them myself. One good thing about the Mid-Main Fair was that the FCA agreed to process any sales with VISA or MasterCard in exchange for a 10 percent fee. This worked for me, as the one sale I had was a VISA charge. I don't do enough sales to warrant my own VISA account, so the FCA's help was really valuable.

How do you promote yourself?

On all the artworks I sell, I include an "about the artist" and "about the artwork" sheet as well as contact info. People like to know a story. They don't seem to trust their own ability to look at something and go "Wow that's really good!" They need to be told what it is, and that's one thing doing a show gets you—the opportunity to tell stories. I take along a little piece of etching plate and explain how I do them; the plate and my process fascinates visitors.

One of the other things I do is I give away art stamps. I sort of miniaturize my work and put a little bowl of them out, and people can help themselves. They're free miniaturized laser prints of my drawings or prints.

The primary advertising I do is through my e-newsletter that I send out three to five times a year to a contact list of about 200 people. I have a spreadsheet of folks on my list with columns for each mailing, so that I can track who got what.

Also, I'm a member of the Architectural Institute of BC, Malaspina Printmakers, Federation of Canadian Artists, and the Alcuin Society. All of these groups have their own mailing lists, journals, eNews, websites, blogs etcetera, and I get them to publicize my shows. The AIBC, for example, sent out three e-news blasts during my *Septessence* show to about 2,300 members, and their blasts and website both had a live link to my web page.

EPILOGUE

In my courses at Emily Carr University each term, my greatest wish is that my students understand the power of a good mailing list and the importance of designing an excellent communications strategy to apply to its members. You should aim to have a large mailing list of people to whom you can send such compelling communications that they want to own your work—to have a piece of you.

Gary is a master of this aspect of his practice. He has developed a very strong and fulfilling part-time creative practice for himself. When he retires, he will have a business to provide him with a vital source of post-retirement income.

CONSIDERING THE GENDER OF ART BUYERS

Off the record, after our interview concluded, I raised a subject provoked by his art and my new understanding of how he markets it.

In my art-teaching experience, perhaps ninety percent of participants are female. When I go to visual art sales events or gallery openings, a greater percentage of men are in attendance, but women far outweigh men in attendance and sales statistics. (You can learn art consumer market information, including demographic information, from Myartclub.com. Their *Canadian Fine Art Market Report 2008* can be downloaded and is valuable reading.)

The imagery in much of Gary's representational artwork is masculine, including boats, fish, heavy machinery, train wrecks, boat wrecks, kayaking and shorelines. This aspect of his work presents a unique marketing opportunity.

Gary mentioned that he has tried advertising in the well-known local visual art publication, *Preview*. He is thinking like most artists do in their approach to marketing, using traditional outlets like galleries and fairs, with one bold difference: His Salon. But even that is a traditional forum for art sale—it's an auction.

I think Gary should consider advertising more to men via media that serve professional mariners, foresters, engineers, etcetera. I'd also suggest he look into what kind of newsletters or magazines serve the local construction industry as a way to meet men who use the equipment he likes to draw. Were I his agent, as part of my marketing strategy for his artwork, I would sell Gary as a "guy's artist." I would choose my language carefully, but I would focus on selling to men and to women who want to buy art for the men in their lives. I believe marketing this way could bring a significant return to Gary, adding to what he already earns in the far more feminized markets he is currently exploiting.

I am not suggesting that Gary only market to men, but that this is something else he could do while continuing what he currently does so well. I think that he would be wise to target male customers as a unique growth strategy appropriate to his practice.

LINKS

Alcuin Society: www.alcuinsociety.com
Architectural Institute of BC: www.aibc.ca
Federation of Canadian Artists: http://artists.ca
Malaspina Printmakers: www.malaspinaprintmakers.com
Preview Magazine: www.preview-art.com

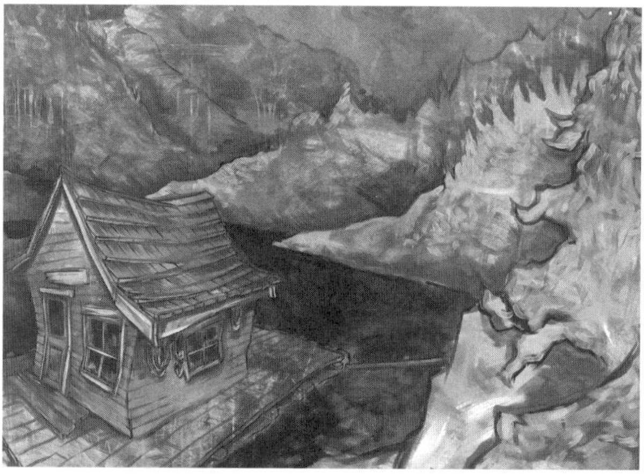

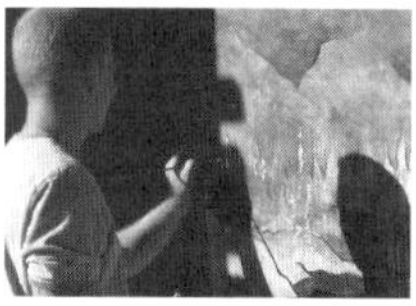

DAVYD ORAM, 1980

At home on the Drifts; acrylic on panel 2010, 96" x 48"

http://www.veniceissinking.com

8 Davyd Oram

Cost Management: Davyd reduces expenses and earns marketing momentum by having a corporate sponsor.

Date of interview: June 10, 2010

"Instead of, 'What can you offer us?' they asked, 'What can we offer you?' And so I asked them to provide me with product to give to my students. They sent me six boxes of pens right away. And then they said, "Let's talk about this; let's cultivate this."

— *Davyd Oram*

PROLOGUE

I met Davyd by email. He wrote to invite me to visit his website, and that led to further correspondence and a discussion about his corporate sponsorship by Sakura of America. I wondered what the term "sponsorship" actually meant in practical terms, and how it worked. It sounded like a good idea, but I was used to sponsorships serving organizations, not individuals.

Another positive impression of Davyd's practice that I got from his website, was in his use of technology for the development of his practice. He lives in a small community, so I knew he was earning income from clients in other towns and cities.

Davyd is a young artist at the beginning of his career. To be earning 100% of his income by making art at so young an age is a significant achievement, especially as he and his partner have a young child; he is a skilled entrepreneur.

The more I learned about Davyd, the more interested I became. On his website, he speaks in a confident, creative voice that seems open to new ideas; he seems both driven to create and yet practical.

I decided to interview him because he is young and because of his street-wise enterprising business acumen. I interviewed Davyd in his home via telephone.

INTERVIEW

How did you get started with visual art?

I've always been an artist. It's been progressive throughout my whole life. When I was a little kid growing up in Sechelt, B.C., I was interested in drawing. My parents gave me my first materials and fostered my development, but then they divorced when I was still very young.

Coming out of a dysfunctional family caused me to spend a lot of time analyzing everything around me. In high school, I didn't apply myself to academics, but I loved making art. My art teacher, Enid Kelly, saw my energy and put the tools in my hand that enabled me to explore and express what I was feeling. Whereas a teacher normally has a curriculum and instructs everyone, Enid just let me go and encouraged me. At the time, I was really a rebellious young kid, but she made me realize my possibilities and that I loved making art. I skipped all my academic classes and was in the art room for five-to-six hours a day. I never once got in trouble for it; I was never suspended or anything. The school even gave me an award for being the most artistic kid in the school. I'm completely self-taught. So I made a list of the artists that I wanted to study and analyzed their careers. I was really into Picasso first, then Dali and Warhol. Enid was the only teacher who invested in me. She even recently invited me to come back and talk to her classes. She's been a mentor and now, as an adult, that process has come full circle with me giving back to her students.

You teach classes for her now?

Yes. I would love to teach in lots of places, but right now it's been local high schools. Soon, though, I'm going to start teaching at elementary schools as well.

What happened after you finished high school?

When I got out of school, I moved to a small town up the coast and started working long hours at a boat yard. I developed a work ethic there that, in the last few years, I've transferred to making art. I'm twenty-nine now, but when I got out of school at seventeen, I worked twelve-hour shifts and then came home to draw. At that time, I was really into making little booklets of my adventures and travels.

You mean graphic novels?

Yes, but this was before computers, so it was all cut and paste and photocopied. I probably made thirty or forty of them, making about fifty copies of each one, and I gave them all away. I was coming out of the punk rock ethic of "do it yourself." What it really did for me was teach me that I could be a part of a community.

Were you still working at the boat yard?

I worked there for five years and then I moved up to Quadra Island for roughly seven years. I moved to the north end of the island where there are only thirty-to-forty people; it's very isolated. I started painting nonstop, probably up to sixteen hours a day. I basically lived money-free, trading labour for everything.

I could devote all my time to working on art on Quadra. Painting was my purpose, and everyone knew it and left me alone to paint. I think by age twenty-five or twenty-six, I'd painted about a thousand paintings, and they were all completed works, they weren't just amateur sketches. In 2006, I had my first show, and I filled it with sixty-four paintings and a big mural—everything that I had done in the previous three years. It was the first time I'd shown my work to the community.

My first accredited show was in the summer of 2007. It was in a professional gallery space in a bigger town, and I was paid an exhibition fee. That experience taught me that art had a power to command an audience, and seeing my own work create my own audience made me think, "Wow, that's quite an accomplishment." So now I dream of being able to buy a house being able to actually raise my family as an artist. And when you're thirty, you start thinking about the retirement plan, and about other things and the challenge just keeps growing.

I read on your website that you are involved in an interesting visual art/music collaboration.

I live in Sechelt now. I left Quadra Island when I met my partner. After I moved here, I met a musician and that led to me going on tour with him. I do live murals during the band's performances. We travelled around B.C. and Alberta at the beginning of 2009.

And how did that pay your bills?

I was hitting a brick wall trying to convince people who had little money to buy $1,500 paintings. It didn't work. So when I moved to Sechelt, where I had a stable studio space and my partner's support, I started to do a lot more research about the business of art. I made friends with a mentor actually—Frank Ogden—who has this persona as Dr. Tomorrow. The guy's done so many random things in his life, but he said to me, "Don't aim for the bottom, aim for the top."

After that, I'd target the people who ran the company when I wanted to get a commission. If they liked my artwork, I'd say, "Why not commission some?" And then things would happen. One company commissioned pieces for their Vancouver office, and then their New York office commissioned a piece, and that led to more commissions. And it was the same with the live murals—the more you do, the more you're wanted.

What percentage of your commissions is the result of you making a proposal to a corporate client?

I would say probably seventy-five to eighty percent. Every now and then you get an unsolicited commission, but everything is a result of successful marketing. I do a lot of cold calls, but if you I find a way in—a name I know or recognize, or the name of somebody I did work for once—it makes the process a lot easier.

When I was on a tour with the musician, we did a performance at Sun Peaks Resort, and their operations manager got a hold of me during the performance and said, "I would really love to bring you back up here to do some murals with a symphony for us this summer." I followed up with Sun Peaks right away, but within two weeks of asking me, the operations manager lost her job. The people that replaced her did not have the experience of seeing me perform the first mural, so I had to really be on the ball to get them to understand the potential. I wound up doing a few performances up there that significantly raised my profile, so now I get $1,500 to paint a mural in an hour and a half, as a performance.

So you have painting commissions, teaching, and painting performances as sources of income. Anything else?

Lately I've been trying to get into the book-illustrator world. I've been pursuing that, plus spending more time doing illustrations. With the paintings, it'll either be for shows or for commissions; the commissions are the most lucrative part of my practice. Doing the musical performance tours puts me in front of a hugely receptive audience, and so whether it's just dropping my name or my website address or something, I put the seed in their head that they can get something from me to remind them of the experience they are having. Sometimes we raffle off my paintings at the end of the night. A random person can win an eight-foot by four-foot painting that they saw completed in front of them.

I did about forty tours over six months, but now I'm focusing on doing murals for charitable organizations because, from a business point of view, doing charitable work puts me in touch with people who have a lot of disposable income plus an interest in art.

Your practice might seem "commercial" to some artists.

My dad was a labour organizer. He was president of the B.C. Ferries union for five years, and he taught me about social justice and, on the other hand, about business. He taught me not to be afraid of being successful. When you hear a word like "entrepreneurial" in relation to art, there's often this huge stigma that you're not supposed to have a business sense. But as a small business owner, which is what you are when you are an artist selling your work, it requires more attentiveness and more enthusiasm.

A clever and unique aspect of your practice is that you have a sponsor.

It's a branch office of Sakura of America. Sakura is a huge brand in Japan. They make these fantastic pens that I started using when I was about twenty years old. I use them to do illustrations because they last forever. They have a beautiful range of tips, they're permanent and they're waterproof—you can paint over them and wash them. They're a phenomenal product, but they're about $8 a pen. For a student artist who's trying to watch the bottom line, buying a whole bunch of these pens is just brutal. But doing some research, I discovered a guy called Dan Price.

Dan came up in the art world because of a great friend who started a shoe company. The friend got Dan to do all the promotional illustrations, the boxes and ads and things like that, in a very simple black-line style. So I looked the guy up in 2005, and on all his work, on the last page, he had a drawing of a pen, and it said "Sakura.com." The Sakura logo was drawn by hand; it didn't look too corporate. So I made a shortlist of the supplies that were expensive for me to buy, and I wrote a letter to each one. I included information about the charitable mural performances I was doing and about my school talks and sent it to about thirty companies. But Sakura was the company I wanted to support me because they are ethical. I thought it was a company with which I could cultivate a business relationship that would be mutually beneficial. And that goes back to Dr. Tomorrow saying, "Always aim for the top, right?"

And Sakura said "Yes" to your proposal?

I didn't get any responses to my emails except from Julie Reed at Sakura. She said, "We loved your work, we loved your story, we love what you're about—that you used our pens almost exclusively for almost a decade. You care about the product. What can we offer you?" Instead of, "What can you offer us?" they asked, "What can we offer you?" And so I asked them to provide me with product to give to my students. They sent me six boxes of pens right away. And then they said, "Let's talk about this; let's cultivate this."

About a month later, I sent them a list of my upcoming events for the next six months, and I got a giant box in the mail because, she said, they don't like sending small packages. Plus, they sent laminated signs that I requested, and a lot of other things from their inventory. My responsibility was to do my performances and classes, show their logo and mention that I'm sponsored by them, plus put their logo on my website—to do cross-promotion. That's how I started doing a lot of this corporate work. The more I learned about business from working with Sakura, the more I learned about corporate promotional write-offs and things like that. In corporate thinking, it's good promotion for many of them to be associated with a rising young artist.

Every month or so, I send Sakura an email, or they send me an email just checking up on things, seeing if anything's needed or in response to the latest set of pictures I have sent to them. By working with me, Sakura has an authority who has learned from experience, speaking knowledgeably about their products to large groups of young people; it's just a complete win-win. And from just a human level, they're putting their support into somebody who's working his butt off to advance his career path. It's a phenomenally good relationship.

EPILOGUE

I did not know that Davyd had suffered as a result of a family break-up, nor that he was disinclined to academics, but it moves me tremendously every time I read or hear about the therapeutic value of artistic self-expression. Davyd's story is valuable for that lesson alone.

But one positive aspect of Davyd's story worth noting is in his acknowledgement of the mentoring he has enjoyed: Enid Kelly and Frank Ogden both played an important role in the narrative of Davyd's life. In virtually every successful artist story that I hear, a parent, teacher or community member has guided, encouraged and respected the artist's creative expression. For parents, this is a valuable lesson: Davyd, like some children, has a brain that does better with images than numbers or letters and deserves to be encouraged and nourished.

Another outstanding aspect of Davyd's story is that he generates "75% to 80%" of his business from commissions. That is a remarkable (and highly efficient) was of operating a practice; in this regard, his practice is reminiscent of the practice of renaissance artists.

Davyd is an adventurous young man, unafraid of risk and driven by passion. He has developed his profession intuitively, focusing on reducing expenses as well as increasing revenues. It was to save money, that Davyd approached Sakura, and it was to save money that he began to barter. The sponsorship idea is a variant of bartering, trading promotion for product. He is a pathological survivor, a positive, self-reliant artist who creates his own success.

BARTERING

Years ago, I met the American painter Tom Lynch. He was a master watercolourist and a dynamic demonstrator and teacher. Teaching was a significant part of his career, and he quickly earned himself a sponsor because he could deliver a lot of "viewer impressions" to the sponsor's marketing department—a vast number of people attended his workshops each year, all over the US.

Tom's non-artistic passion was golf. Wherever he went to teach art classes, he sought out the best golf clubs and traded a beautiful painting of the course's prettiest green in exchange for access to the course while he was in the city. When I met him, he had golfed on many of the most famous courses in the US and Canada.

My own experience with bartering involved a woman named Audrey Skalbania, who ran a restaurant in Stanley Park. She chose me to make her menus, which changed often, and she paid me generously with credit at her restaurant. I used my credits strategically, saving them to impress an important potential client (or favoured regular client) to a nice dinner.

THE ESSENTIAL PREREQUISITE OF A SPONSORSHIP

Philanthropy comes with no strings. Sponsorships usually involve a trade. In exchange for a sponsorship, the sponsor expects as many people as possible to be exposed (as often as possible) to the sponsor's corporate name, logo and/or message. It is the responsibility of the sponsored agent or agency to deliver the "viewer impressions" the sponsor seeks.

When cigarette advertising was banned from print and broadcast media, tobacco companies started paying large sums of money to sponsor the largest-scale sports and cultural events. A visual artist or visual arts organizations can only rarely compete for viewer impressions with performing artists and performing arts producers, whose audiences fill their facilities for months each year. Galleries and artist collectives can, however, attract sponsors when, over time, they amass a large mailing list.

Because their practices involve large numbers of people, savvy visual artists like Davyd and Tom Lynch can attract sponsorships from corporations selling products to visual artists. I can think of nothing more valuable for an artist than a large mailing list comprised of people with whom some kind of relationship has been developed.

Davyd has developed a unique and highly effective way of building his mailing list with the performance painting he does. And he teaches, so he routinely meets countless numbers of students of art. He learned quickly that students do not make great customers—they are too poor—so his practice is moving to a focus on the corporate work he does with charities, where clients with deep pockets are plentiful. Charity work can add valuable contacts to your list.

Not every artist can attract (or has interest in) a corporate sponsorship. For many, it may seem improbable or irrelevant, but there are many different forms of corporate sponsorships between artists and corporations. In some ways, I see corporations today as the equivalent of the aristocratic, clerical or academic patrons and mentors of the past, who so influenced the lives of great artists through patronage.

LINKS

Sakura: www.sakuraofamerica.com

Tom Lynch: www.tomlynch.com

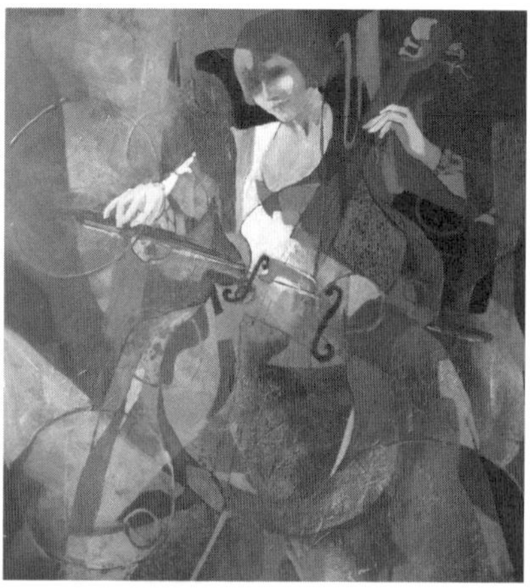

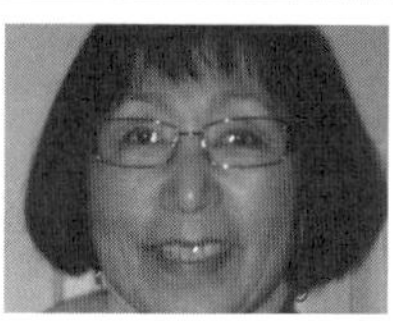

JOYCE KAMIKURA, 1942

Adagio; acrylic on canvas

2110, 36" x 30"

http://joycekamikura.blogspot.com

9 Joyce Kamikura

Licensing: Joyce successfully sold the reproduction rights to several of her works (but had some surprising outcomes).

Date of interview: October 5, 2010

"I was happy that I had a voice in choosing my paintings for publication. Soon though, I realized I was operating under a false illusion of what would sell. I was naive to think that good works sell to the mass market."

— *Joyce Kamikura*

PROLOGUE

Selling the reproduction rights to your artwork can earn you a substantial financial return, but it can also be a challenging emotional and/or legal experience. Just as the process of choosing a gallery to represent you can be an onerous decision, so can the choosing of a publisher. Your relationship with both types of agent requires complete trust and openness, because once you enter into a contractual relationship with an agent, it can be hard to endure and/or terminate.

It all comes down to the contract. Artists often sign disadvantageous contracts because they succumb to emotional decision-making; the artists' strong desire to be represented or published leads them to sign contracts that are developed by, and favour, the publisher. We can hurry into a decision without doing proper due diligence. Contracts can be intentionally or unintentionally confusing, depending on the integrity of the contractor and their consulting lawyers. Consequently, it is imperative that you understand *every single clause*, as well as your rights and the conventions of the fine art licensing industry.

Understanding the clauses of a publisher's contract written by a corporate lawyer is usually beyond a layperson. Anyone entering into a licensing agreement would be wise to consult a contract lawyer; the greater the potential for return, and/or the larger the publisher, the more important it is for you to have a legal opinion from someone who works for *you*.

If having a work published is of interest to you, there are many resources that are easily accessible. Foremost is Google. Just type "art licensing" (or an equivalent) into Google to be overwhelmed by information. Another valuable resource is the CARFAC Copyright Collective website. It is a rich resource specifically for Canadian artists. And finally, perhaps the best resource is an experienced peer, and that is why I arranged to interview Joyce.

Please note that in this chapter, we are talking about the licensing of images for the purpose of making reproductions and *not* prints. Artist "prints" are made by hand and numbered as part of a limited edition series. Reproductions are commercial mass-production lithographs, which is what Joyce did.

I visited Joyce in her home in Richmond, B.C., to talk about her experience with publishers of reproductions.

INTERVIEW

Do you remember when you first got interested in creating visual art?

I was in high school in Montreal when I became interested in art, especially in painting. I wanted to become an artist but my parents didn't allow me to pursue it. I was told, "Just go to university and take whatever you want, except art." Since I didn't have any science background through high school, there were only two faculties at U.B.C. that allowed someone with a non-science background to enter, and one of them was Commerce. It was a five-year course at the time. The other was probably art, but I felt that I had no choice in the matter and enrolled in the Commerce Faculty.

Were you making art while you were studying in college?

There was no time for studying or practicing art. After getting my Commerce degree, marrying and having a family, I decided to go to art school. By this time, my kids were in their early teens and the closest art school was Kwantlen College in Surrey, so I went there to take some courses for two to three years. After that, I earned admission directly into the fourth year of the Langara College program, where I could study under Leslie Poole. I only took courses that interested me—art history, design, drawing, and painting.

Was anyone encouraging your decision to study fine art?

Not at all. But in a seminar I was in, one of the students owned a gallery. It was the Creek House Gallery on Granville Island, in Vancouver. She took an interest in my work and asked me to show with her. So I got started right away with a gallery, and that was encouraging.

Did your work sell well?

It was steady, and then one day I got a call from Gary Peters of Art In Motion. He saw my paintings at Creekhouse and asked if I was interested in reproducing some of them. Initially, my answer was no. I'd had past experience with a card company that reproduced one of my images, and all I got out of it was a bunch of cards and a token royalty. So I told Gary that I wasn't interested unless he was going to promote me as an artist; I did not want to be part of the piece-by-piece marketing of my work. He said he would promote me as an artist, as well as promoting each image printed. We agreed on the terms for our contract, and he chose four pieces to publish. My works were an huge hit here and at the New York and California trade fairs!

The first agreement that you made with Art in Motion was for four pieces?

The initial agreement was for the exclusive right to publish my work. At first they just chose four, but they had the right to more. After the success of my work at international trade shows, they printed many more different images in succession.

Did you trust Art in Motion or did you have a lawyer look at the agreement?

I discussed it with my husband who is an accountant. He's very careful about wording in documents. I felt very fortunate to have the agreement almost exactly as I wished.

Was payment based on how many works were printed, or purchased?

On how many the company sold, and my royalties were based on the wholesale price.

And how did you know how many sold?

I had to rely on his honesty.

You had no way of checking?

No. Not unless I asked to see the books. I was earning quite a bit of money at the time, and I trusted that they were giving me the right amount.

Were you still exhibiting with Creekhouse Gallery?

Yes.

Did you retain the original work and the right to sell it?

Yes I did, and some originals were bought by Art in Motion.

Do you have any idea of the volumes that were sold?

Thousands per image. They went so well that Art in Motion offered them in different sizes, including art cards.

And when did you enter into the agreement with Art in Motion?

I would say twenty-five to thirty years ago. This was when Art in Motion was just struggling to make their presence known in the international market place. I grew up with Art in Motion. I stayed with them for about fifteen years. Then I went to Canadian Art Prints.

Why did you switch to Canadian Art Prints?

I was of the impression that I could influence these companies to pick what I thought were my better pieces. The pieces that Art in Motion chose were not, in my opinion, my best. I was not proud to say, when I saw them, "Hey, I did those paintings;" not all of them, anyway. Some of my best pieces wouldn't get picked for publication.

Did Canadian Art Prints give you a voice in determining which of your prints were published?

Yes, but only initially. I was happy that I had a voice in choosing my paintings for publication. Soon though, I realized I was operating under a false illusion of what would sell. I was näive to think that good works sell to the mass market. I realized that the printing companies are the experts on marketing to mass media.

What determines what publishers choose?

I know many artists who are way more skilful than I am, but I was lucky to be there at the right time, for the right market. My paintings happened to have the colour, image and ambience that they were looking for at the time. Your works can be chosen because of these kinds of reasons, over technical and creative talent. What they are looking for — color, image, softness, hardness or whatever— changes constantly, from season to season, and from year-to-year.

In your case, they approached you, as opposed to you approaching a publisher, correct?

At the point in my art career when they approached me, I would never have taken the publication route. I didn't know the business at all. Remember, in the 80's, publication technology was not as developed as it is today, and it was extremely difficult and expensive for an individual to publish his or her own works and market them. I think many artists who want to be published by a third party give up too easily. I try to encourage them, when they submit their pieces to publishers, not to give up. You have to keep sending your work out because, depending on the flavour of the day, publishers might be looking for something that they rejected earlier. Colour is everything to publishers; first the colour, then the image—that is my impression. You might have a very good piece that's marketable, but the colour may not be the colour of the day; you won't know why they didn't choose your work, so you just have to keep submitting. Today's submission process is so much easier than when I was submitting many years ago. Now you can send your images by email.

Is the fine art reproduction market thriving?

It's a huge business, but in most cases artists get very little monetary reward unless they are willing to deal with the mass market. It's posters that make money, apparently. My latest by Canadian Art Prints were a combination of posters and giclées printed on canvas; they decide what format they're going to use.

How often does your publisher provide you with a sales report?

Every month. And sometimes the cheques are in American funds. That's nice when the exchange is good.

Are you still with Canadian Art prints?

Yes, but I haven't had any prints done for a long time.

Are they still handling stock that they licensed in the past?

That's right.

But they're not taking new work?

Not for a while, they haven't.

Have you ever published your own giclée prints?

I tried it, but it was a total flop. The cost of making them is very high. Even though I studied marketing when I was in Commerce at UBC, I did absolutely no marketing research before I decided to do them. I wanted to go into giclées because I had built myself a website, and I'd paid a lot for its development. Also, on the one hand, I had very expensive paintings, and on the other, very inexpensive reproductions; I had nothing in between. So I thought doing giclée prints would be the answer, giving me some products priced in between. But after I'd had them done, I realized that using my website alone was not going to sell them.

Only one of my regular gallery agents was willing to market my giclées. They sold a couple, but that was it. I lost money venturing into a market I knew nothing about; it was something I could not handle. Keeping my web site was expensive and time-consuming, and I wasn't selling any work through it, so I decided to shut it down in spite of having spent six months building it. I decided to concentrate on creating art and leave the marketing of my works to professional agents.

Have you developed other ways to earn income then?

Commercial galleries are my true agents; they are an important source of income for me. Workshops were another income source; I was invited to do workshops by art clubs and associations in both Canada and the U.S. And Art rentals is another. I rent my work through the Vancouver Art Gallery's Sales and Rentals program; I've been doing it for years, and going by the cheques, they seem to be constantly rented out. Once in a while, I change the paintings—maybe every three years, in case the renters get tired of seeing the same work. Sometimes a renter buys a piece, so you get rental income for a while, plus a sale. I also rent to movies. There are a lot of movies made in Vancouver. I'm not with Artworks anymore, but when I was with them, they were constantly renting out my originals to movies. Again, you get small cheques now and then.

Do they take a commission if they sell?

Yes, that's right. They take a commission on rentals, too.

Getting back to your painting, did you remain with Creekhouse Gallery until they closed?

Yes, and by then, because of the popularity of my prints, I didn't have to search for galleries any more; they came to me. I had enough galleries representing me.

And how many galleries were you in at that time?

I was in about five-or-six galleries (in different cities). Exhibiting originals and licensing prints go hand-in-hand—because the prints were popular, people thought the originals must be good paintings, and so my originals sold well too. And now that I'm not into printing work that much, the originals require much more sophisticated buyers. I feel my recent paintings are much more creative, better executed and truthful, so they require more educated eyes to be appreciated.

Has your output diminished as you have aged?

Yes. I'm not as ambitious as before. I find solo shows really stressful. I'm at the point where I do what I want and am proud of my creative accomplishments, regardless of the marketability of the work. I don't want to be an "I saw your beautiful print in Stockholm" kind of artist. I want to create images to *my* satisfaction.

Different artists have different goals in life. When people say to me that I am a successful artist, I think they mean financially successful. My income from reproductions was, at its height around twenty-five years ago, very high by any standard. It was unbelievable! And I threw it all out to go to another company because I wasn't happy with the choice of images being reproduced. It was important to succeed financially as an artist, but after a certain length of time, something else becomes more important. I want to do the best I can as an artist, and not be so focused on financial success. Who knows, the two may meet one day.

What would you say to emerging artists about a career in the arts?

That it's a tough business to be in—but I guess they know that. I would say to be practical about marketing their stuff—especially, initially. Eventually, satisfaction as an artist will be realized if you're truthful to yourself in creating. Creating for the market may be a necessity for you, but while you're doing so, I suggest you create for yourself.

EPILOGUE

Below are some generalizations about how publishers choose the images they publish, gleaned from conversations I have had with published artists and from perusing the websites of fine art publishers:

1. **Imagery**: Publishers clearly prefer representational work. Abstract work is harder to sell. Like the publishers, art consumers in the general population prefer subject material that can be "understood." And further, I would say that publishers want images that tend toward the non-specific or generic. The market seems to be dominated by imagery designed to appeal to our emotions or that are "attractive." Reproductions tend to be decorative and can often be categorized as sentimental.
2. **Imagery**: Iconic imagery is preferred. What is iconic is a highly subjective decision; what is iconic in other communities (or markets) is likely to include different imagery than your home community. Try to talk with the publishers who interest you (or their artists), to help you focus on subjects that will increase your chances of creating imagery that will be published.
3. **Imagery**: Floating imagery seems to sell only to niche markets. By nature, niche markets are small, and publishers of visual art reproductions want the largest markets possible, so images that fill the canvas or paper, far outnumber images that present a "floating" image on a background of a single tone and colour. Floating images feel more like posters or illustrations than fine art.
4. **Imagery**: My impression is that the majority of images reproduced seem targeted to women. Women dominate domestic decision-making, and since artwork reproductions are largely used for interior design, imagery that can appeal to women does well.
5. **Series**: Your chances of being selected for publication seem better if you submit a series rather than a single image. This is *not* to say that you should submit any four images; you should submit a series of four images that relate to each other in a perceivable way. If you visit publishing websites, you will see many items in series, which allows customers to buy a single image, a pair or the series.
6. **Composition**: Works with a clear focal interest seem more likely to succeed, based on sales analyses, as does work where the focus dom-

inates the composition. Further, work in a 3:4 horizontal ratio dominates the market. Works that are 8" X 12" or 18" X 24" seem to be most popular, and fit standard frames.

7. **Texture**: Textured work is hard to reproduce effectively, if the texture contributes to the impression of the piece. So textured work is less likely to be selected for publication. Submit work that is not textured and rich in colour. Work that is rich in colour outsells works with a palette limited in colour or tone. Black and white work is not popular on art reproductions websites.

Nothing beats doing a little research. Spend some time on Google, and visit the sites of art publishers. You will learn a lot. Insightful resources for Canadians are the Art in Motion website and the Canadian Art Prints website (see page 121). However, the licensing of visual art moves easily across borders and into far larger markets than Canada, so if you are interested in licensing your work, research international art reproduction publishers.

KNOW YOUR RIGHTS

Canadian artists are very lucky to have the Canadian Artists Representation Copyright Collective Inc. (CARCC) at their disposal. CARCC is a society, born of, and affiliate to, Canadian Artists' Representation (a separate society and the national service organization for Canadian visual artists). The following text is from the CARFAC website:

"CARCC, established in 1990, is a copyright collective that licenses and administers copyright for visual and media artists in Canada. [It] is a subsidiary organization of CARFAC [....]

"Affiliates or members of CARCC (artists) assign their copyrights to CARCC for licensing and administration. All uses of a CARCC member's copyright must be licensed by CARCC.

"Some of the copyrights administered by CARCC are: Exhibition, ***reproduction***, reprography and telecommunication. In addition to representing living artists, CARCC represents artists' estates. In Canada, most copyrights endure for the artist's lifetime plus fifty years. Moral rights endure for the same length of time.

"Copyright fees are increasingly becoming a necessary and major source of income for visual artists. Copyright is not transferred upon the sale of a work; copyright is retained by the artist unless specifically and separately sold, and the artist can continue to generate copyright revenue from the work after the work itself is sold or donated."

For further information about CARFAC, CARCC and your rights, I encourage you to visit their websites. If you are interested in licensing the reproduction of your work, you *must* know your rights and protect them.

LINKS

Art in Motion: www.artinmotion.com

Canadian Art Prints: www.canadianartprints.com

CARFAC Copyright Collective: www.carcc.ca

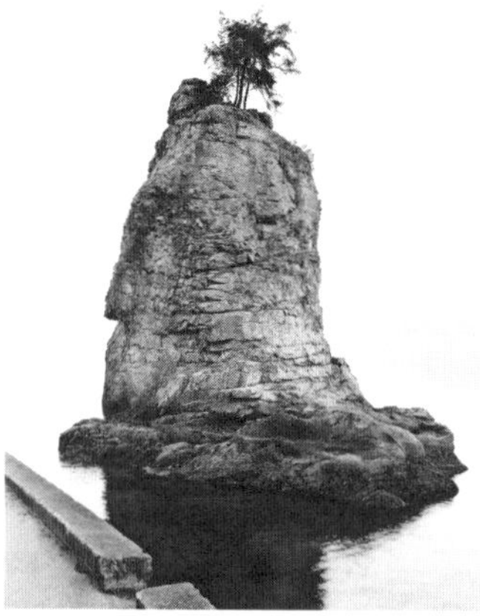

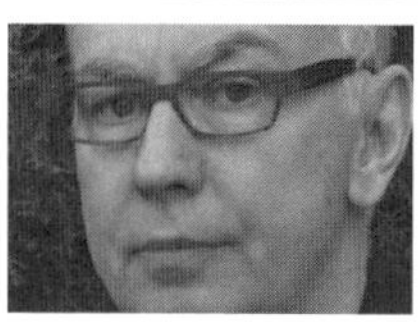

LEE BACCHUS, 1950

Siwash Rock, 2005

http://splinterinyoureye.blogspot.com

10 Lee Bacchus

Bartering: Lee partnered with another artist to get the marketing services he needed.

Date of interview: August 12, 2010

"I knew that it was going to be a lot of work, and I told Brian right at the beginning that I wasn't going to do it unless he agreed to do the selling to distributors. I'm not good at that; he's much more a people person."

— *Lee Bacchus*

PROLOGUE

Close your eyes and visualize a "typical artist." Next, conjure up the image of an "entrepreneur." Are the two images vastly different? What are the striking differences between the two images/people that your imagination conjures in response to my requests?

In my teaching, I find that there is a considerable divergence in the images conjured up by these two words and the difference in our perceptions of these two professionals fuels insightful conversations. If you want to successfully sell your work, if you want to live exclusively as an artist, you must be able to picture yourself in both roles.

Social theorists say that a high percentage of people who self-identify as artists think of themselves as introverts. Business theorists say that extroversion is a valuable asset because extroverts enjoy a strong sense of self-confidence, are highly skilled communicators and can project absolute conviction in their goals. Both artists and entrepreneurs are creative innovators and take risks, but if you are introverted or shy, you face more of a challenge in the marketplace than your extroverted peers.

The history of art includes many extroverted, charismatic innovators who achieved enormous wealth and fame. Most of my experience, however, is with artists who find self-advocacy supremely challenging. Consequently, any innovative and productive sales methodology that's particularly suited to introverts interests me.

Obviously, one way introverted artists can deal with sales is to seek representation with a commercial art gallery. Representation is viewed by many artists as the ideal solution to their disinclination to sales, but this attitude reveals a naïve view of the relationship between artists and their galleries. Artists exhibiting in commercial galleries should be actively involved in the sale of their work. You cannot abrogate your sales responsibilities to a gallery or any agent if you want to participate successfully in the marketplace. You must be entrepreneurial *with* your gallerist.

Each artist can find a way suited to his or her temperament to relate to the market. So, when the proprietor of an eclectic Vancouver store told me the back story of the photographs hanging for sale on her wall, I knew I wanted to talk to the photographer.

I interviewed photographer and writer Lee Bacchus by telephone.

INTERVIEW

How did your career begin?

I was a journalist at the *Vancouver Sun* and *Province* newspapers for twenty years. During that time I'd been interested in photography, but it was during the last ten years that I started taking photography more seriously—it was something I had done as a hobby most of my life. Then, when I thought I was a better photographer, I started doing some freelancing for *Vancouver Magazine*, submitting images accompanied by articles that I had written.

Were you freelancing while working at the newspaper?

Yes. The paper had the right to first refusal of the ideas I proposed, but all my stories were either too lengthy or too peculiar for them. I knew the paper wouldn't be interested in them.

And you no longer work for a newspaper?

I quit in 2003. To be honest, at first there wasn't very much work available for me. I only did three or four magazine shoots a year, something like that. But at the same time, I was doing more exploratory work, trying to see what I could come up with that was unique. I studied a lot of the art photographers of the time, and tried to emulate certain things they were doing to see if their techniques would work for me.

And did you show or sell any of that work?

In 2000, I wanted to learn about portraiture. So, through a friend, I got to know people at a halfway house in the Downtown Eastside (of Vancouver) and I started shooting a lot of portraits of people there. Eventually I had two exhibitions that were charity events. They were not curated shows, they were fundraisers, but the response was good.

I was really happy about people's response to my work. It spurred me to keep going, but I turned away from that kind of work. I felt that even though I was doing it in good faith and I was selling the prints to help people, what I was doing felt a little bit exploitive to me. My photography went in a different direction after that.

How did your work change?

It was all over the place until 2004 or 2005, when my friend Brian and I decided that it would be interesting to do a series of postcards of Vancouver—but in a way that isn't so "eye-candy-ish" as what you see in tourist outlets. We didn't want to do the classic views: Totem poles, the suspension bridge, Gastown clock—all the cliché Vancouver images. We wanted to go for a completely different look. For one, we did them in black and white and basically void of people. They were of places you would not normally see on a postcard; there were a couple of familiar sites, but always from a unique perspective. Ultimately, we printed twelve postcards.

How did the partnering on this project work?

We both did a *lot* of work. We basically had a division of labour, although we'd both go out to do the shoot collaboratively. I had a lot more technical knowledge and post-production experience on the computer than Brian, but we would scout places together and talk about how we wanted to shoot them. Ultimately, I would shoot the film and do the production work, and Brian agreed that he would do the marketing. It worked out well for us, because he could go around to places that he thought would be interested in carrying our postcards, and I couldn't do that. He often went in "cold."

Did you use the postcard images in any other ways?

Because we had taken them with a large format camera, it was sort of silly to be making postcards, but I was kind of obsessed with the look of large format images—the true perspective of things, the detail and tones. Then the postcards just ran out of steam. We sold a lot of them at first, but it was a lot of work getting them distributed. They are still selling though. We just sold several to a development company that wanted to give them away as gifts to their new presidents.

Did Brian arrange that, too?

The request actually came to me, but I directed it to Brian. He still handles all the business negotiations. Requests come from people who have seen our blog or our postcards and want large prints of our work. Also, a couple of places started selling large prints. There are a few venues that display our prints permanently, and they work as promotion of our work.

Do you and Brian share a corporate entity that owns your work?

No. We never formed a company or anything. Our arrangement is very informal. We didn't sit down and write out a business model or anything. We sat in a coffee shop and said, "I'll do this and you'll do that;" we really didn't know where it was going to go. We almost panicked at the point of the publication of the postcards when we had to pay the printer; we wondered what we had done.

Was the initial investment a challenge?

It was only a couple of thousand dollars, but we were nervous about selling enough of them to recover our costs. Now that we've made a good return on our investment, I can say that it has worked out very well, but it's mainly because of the prints. We did sell quite a few of the postcards—we probably made our money back on them—but we made the majority of our money from the prints. We shot everything in colour, and then I transferred the images to black and white for the postcards. We have a lot of options because they were shot with such a big camera; we can actually make them wall-to-wall size.

And you share revenues, fifty-fifty?

Yes. When work is sold, we divide what we earn right down the middle. It's just too much work for each of us to tally up all our individual costs; we just think of it as a modest enterprise and share joint ownership of the work.

But the division of labour suited your respective personalities?

From the beginning, my job was all the technical work with the photography. I had the equipment, and I knew how to use it. I do all the post-production work with Photoshop and all the printing. I knew that it was going to be a lot of work, and I told Brian right at the beginning that I wasn't going to do it unless he agreed to do the selling to distributors. I'm not good at that; he's much more a people person.

I think Brian got burned out at a certain point, though. He had a lot more time in those days and did a lot of work, but we weren't making a living off of it. Then he had to return to work; he had taken a sabbatical and had to return to his teaching duties. From then on, we basically worked "on request." We sell a lot through a framing store on Commercial Drive called Artrageous; they display our work nicely and sometimes do window displays of our work. The owner keeps tab of what he owes us, and we get things framed there, so it's almost like a bartering system. It's a good arrangement for us, because we frame a lot of the larger format photographs there.

With Brian back at teaching, could future projects have a different partner?

I'm not sure. Brian and I were friends as children and are very close. We think alike, but collaboration, even with Brian, can be very fractious at times. Each person has his own idea of what something should do or be. I know there were a few times when it got pretty tense between us, but I would never have done it with someone else. As far as any future marketing and sales is concerned, for me, it would have to be with people and places that Brian has already established relationships with. I can't go out and find new places to sell work.

You're saying that it's not an easy thing to find a partner?

I think you have to find someone who's aesthetically in tune with you, which Brian and I were. We easily agreed on the treatment of an image, whereas another person might not be so accommodating. We could each have done our own separate series of images, separating our aesthetic ideas, but that's not the way we chose to do it. Towards the end, however, we concluded that were we to go further with the project, it would probably be best to go that route.

So, a couple of years back you produced a large body of work with Brian, and it continues to provide both of you with income and opportunities.

Exactly. It's like getting royalties. We spent probably close to a year producing the work, and there are many that we didn't use on the postcards. We don't earn a lot, but it's nice, every once in a while, to earn some revenue from our investment.

EPILOGUE

In wanting to sell his work, Lee faced several challenges: His introversion, a lot of competition, and, because the market for photography is not strong and most commercial galleries focus on paintings, few obvious outlets. The success of his methodology, therefore, is significant and has a "long tail," in that it is still earning him income and commissions.

In the interview, Lee identified himself as an introvert. The social demands and self-advocacy required to establish a network of consignment outlets for an artist/photographer can be daunting, particularly for an introvert. Lee's intuitive and creative solution, to work with Brian, is a good model for artist-introverts to consider. I would, however, recommend that some kind of agreement be established between you and any potential partner. Whereas Lee and Brian had an informal arrangement, it is not a professional partnership model.

I played a minor role in the development of another model of a partnership. It involved three women artists whom I met when they rented studios in a downtown Vancouver warehouse I was managing. They hired me to participate in a discussion about how the three of them might best increase sales of their work. Each was uncomfortable with self-advocacy; one said she felt far more comfortable selling her friends' work, than her own. After that comment, talk focused more on how each could promote the work of the other two.

Finding inspiration in two popular movies, they named themselves Easel's Angels and started an informal collaboration and set out to conquer visual art wholesaling. (The Easel's Angels name was an inside private joke; they did not use this name publicly.) They decided to approach the challenge of obtaining consignment agreements for their work together, instead of individually, and to do so with the kind of female camaraderie seen in two movies: *Sex in the City* and *Charlie's Angels*.

They made a list of potential retail outlets whom they thought might wholesale their work, and each person was responsible for securing an interviews with two stores on the list. They were able to schedule several interviews on each of three consecutive days. When the interview days came, they were ready. They had their hair done, they dressed to impress, and they launched each day of the three-day intensive with a motivational "power breakfast" together.

The good news: Sales far exceeded their expectations. The bad news: All the buyers only selected work by two of the women. Still, they all felt they benefited from the exercise—even the artist whose work did not attract interest felt the days spent together were valuable. She was thrilled with the outcome for her friends and she used the lack of response as motivation for a change in her work. They all agreed that approaching marketing together was infinitely more fun and productive than doing it alone.

Each of these partnership models is a creative solution that worked for the individuals involved, and each methodology was an intuitive solution designed to compensate for the artists' negative attitudes towards self-advocacy, marketing and sales. There's a way for everyone to deal with the challenge of marketing. To find one that works for you or to find help facing any challenge that you have developing your career, get involved in a fellowship of artists. Online or in your community, become involved with a group of artists and find others with whom to network to find innovative ways to work together to further individual sales.

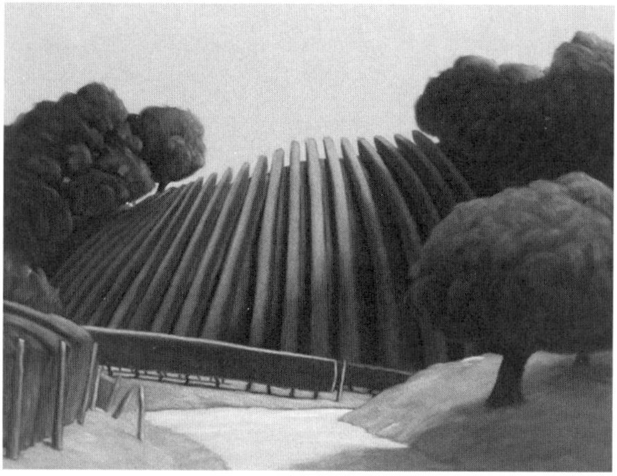

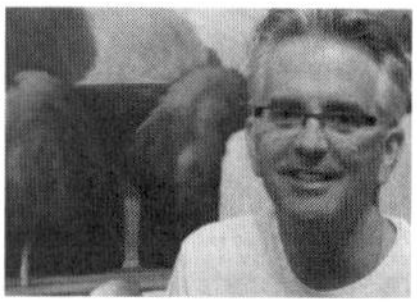

ROSS PENHALL, 1959

Vineyard #1; oil on canvas

2010; 48"x60"

www.rosspenhall.com

11 Ross Penhall

Change: Ross substantially grew his practice through a strategic change of medium.

Date of interview: May 10, 2010

"The first show I had was with another artist, and my half of the gallery sold out. And every show after that, until the economic collapse, sold out; some before the show, some in nine minutes and some with line-ups. It was this crazy thing and entirely unexpected."

— *Ross Penhall*

PROLOGUE

I first noticed the work of Ross Penhall at a small gallery called Paperworks on Granville Island in Vancouver. I liked the fact that he was working with coloured pencil crayons, my preferred creative medium, and was even more intrigued when I learned that he was also a fire-fighter.

Ross drew, and now paints, landscapes. His images feel entirely contemporary, but the absence of the human form adds a strong emotional element. Nature is celebrated in Ross' work; he represents nature's design in a way that reminds me of the reverential and dramatic presentation of tree and sky in the work of Emily Carr.

Several years after first seeing his work, I introduced him to artist and paint maker, Robert Gamblin. Robert is the founder of Gamblin Paints in Oregon and was visiting Vancouver when Ross requested the introduction. When I realized that Ross was painting, and it made me wonder about why Ross would change from using a tight, controlled and slow medium to a far more relaxed, looser and quicker approach to the making of art.

Sometime thereafter, as I was driving down Vancouver's major downtown thoroughfare, Georgia Street, I saw Ross' name and work spectacularly displayed in the front window of Buschlen Mowatt Gallery. The next day, I read in the newspaper that Ross' show had sold out and that people had camped overnight outside the gallery in order to buy one his works. The change in medium appeared to have facilitated a graduation to the more prestigious gallery and much higher prices for his work.

In order to find out what the change in medium had meant to the development and dramatic advancement of Ross' career, I talked with him at Emily Carr University.

INTERVIEW

As a child, did you consider a career as an artist?

I started drawing when I went to Camp Potlatch in Howe Sound. I decided to sketch all the buildings in the camp, while all the other kids went off to draw the plants and things we were supposed to draw. I had my first art show there.

Later, making a living from my art was too big an idea to consider. The thought never even crossed my mind—all I wanted to do was make art. As a young boy, I wanted to draw, and sketch. As a late teen, I wanted to create prints at Malaspina Printmakers and be able to say, at the end of the day, that I was an artist. I wanted to express how good that made me feel rather than figure out how I was going to get paid.

My parents were very supportive. My mother was especially supportive; she loved drawing. I wasn't the best public school student. I was very distracted and easily bored. But art was something that could hold my attention; I wanted to work at it and dedicate time to it.

But you became a firefighter.

I have two distinct sides to my personality. I was twenty-one when I joined the fire department. Being a firefighter appealed to the adventurous side of me, and it gave me a lot of time off. I liked the excitement and thrill of firefighting and serving as a first responder. Fortunately, firefighting was also an honest way to make a salary. Art was a counterbalance. I was always making art, but my approach was scattered. Making it, however, fulfilled me. People would say, "Wow, I love what you do!" And it just grew and grew and grew; I did more and more drawing, and I started having shows in municipal and public galleries. I got my start in the West Vancouver Public Library.

I first saw your work at Paperworks on Granville Island. How would you describe your career at that time?

I was drawing. I was working with graphite, watercolor, colored pencil crayon and printmaking. I was comfortable with drawing. I liked slowly building up layers and cross-hatching with pen and ink.

Did you pursue any training in art?

Yes. I took courses at Capilano College, Emily Carr University and Malaspina Printmakers. As well, I committed to my art, daily. I was not the best art student in high school but I had drive. Art came to me naturally and sincerely; I poured my heart and soul into it. Consequently, my brushwork strengthened and I developed a style.

It really was the desire to do it—to do it every day. I'd go into the studio every day, even if I didn't feel like it, and I'd figure out what I needed to do;

it would come to me. Whatever I needed to do, I'd do. If I didn't feel like painting, I'd prime canvas.

Another factor of your success may be your story. Being a firefighter seems to add to public interest in you as an artist.

Part of being a successful artist is that you're a "package." You need to be many things; you need to be presentable, you need to be personable and you need to treat your collectors well. Fortunately, I had a lot of friends in Vancouver; I've lived here all my life and was well established.

There needs to be a story to go along with your work—I mean, it helps. The work is beautiful on the wall and everything, but there needs to be a story. Oliver (Ross's agent) will call and say that people have come into the gallery and want to know something about me. People want to know the artist; they want a story.

And then, in spite of the success you were having with your drawings, you decided to change what you were doing. What made you do that?

I give my wife, Caron, credit for that. She said to me, "Your works are beautiful, Ross, but they need to be this big." (His hands spread wide apart.) She noticed I was spending a lot of time on these tiny drawings.

My drawings were small, but I was kind of afraid of switching mediums. I'd been trying things like oil pastels, and I was inching my way toward painting—acrylic or oil—but I was afraid. I had a fear of failure perhaps; I thought maybe I couldn't do it, so I decided to learn about the technical side of painting. I went to Emily Carr University's Continuing Studies program and took a course in painting with Lucy Hogg: I read books and studied the work of other artists.

Also, there were certain galleries that I wanted to show in; I wanted to be in a *painting* gallery. And I wanted to see my work bigger, not just because it would sell for more, but because I wanted to paint. A pencil point can feel stifling to me; part of what I wanted to do was speed up. I still draw and do etchings, but painting allows me a greater freedom, wild motion and spontaneity.

I loosened up my style as my career advanced. Presently, I'm not sketching as much; I'm just doing brushwork. I am trying to get away from the pencil point. I'll use a pencil now and then to compose something quickly, but mostly I sketch on the canvas with a brush. I used to plan each image a lot more, but now I think I'm more confident. I like the wide brush and laying in the colors and tonal areas. It's less about line and more about shapes now.

Was it easy to make the change?

I just started painting; I had a style and an idea of how I wanted to paint. At first I didn't quite know how to get there technically, but I learned quickly. I painted about a dozen paintings and gave them to a few auctions, and to friends, and the response was reinforcing. So, with all the courage I could muster, I took a couple of paintings into the Buschlen Mowatt Gallery and showed Ingunn Kemble. She said, "Okay, show me twenty more."

The second time I went in, about a month-and-a-half later, I hadn't done the twenty more paintings but I took in a couple of new paintings for Ingunn and her staff to see. Barry Mowatt, the gallery owner, was there, and he was not one hundred percent sure about them, but the staff thought they were great. Barry asked me, "What do you want from us?" and all I could think of to say was: "Hang my work in the front window!" Then he asked me what I sold my work for, and I told him. Then he asked the staff if they could double the price (at that point of his career, Ross was selling his early paintings at $1,000 – $2,000 per canvas) and they said: "Not a problem. Not a problem." I chose Buschlen Mowatt because I liked the other artists represented there and, at the time, it was a very painterly gallery.

That is the "dream come true" scenario for an artist, isn't it? You did not have to double your sales to retain your accustomed income level, as a result of securing representation.

I didn't really have an income from art at that time. I was a firefighter. It was the early 90s.

But you did get an offer to be represented in a way that had no impact on your net income per canvas. You'd clearly been undervaluing your work in this market, in the opinion of the gallery staff.

Yes, I suppose, but the gallery's endorsement gave me more than money—it gave me confidence in my work. Luckily, I got into the Buschlen Mowatt early in my career. It was good timing. Maybe my twenty years of drawing had prepared me to switch to painting, but I hadn't really been painting that long when they accepted me. It had been less than a year.

You said that part of your original motivation in becoming an artist was the positive feedback, so being accepted by Buschlen Mowatt really must have given you a strong sense of approval.

Absolutely! And I was ready for it. The first show I had was with another artist, and my half of the gallery sold out. And every show after that, until the economic collapse, sold out; some before the show, some in nine minutes and some with line-ups. It was this crazy thing and entirely unexpected.

What was the impact of your success?

It was huge, and a blessing and a curse. It allowed my wife to stop working and focus on the kids. I have a very understanding wife who supports my career choice; she understands the torment, the need and the drive an artist can have. Her involvement with our kids allowed me to spend a lot of time on two careers.

Also, I incorporated. I got some really great advice years ago to incorporate, and I established a family trust. My art has been able to pay for child programming and all the post-secondary education of our kids. As well, I've been able to buy real estate, including my studio.

That must have been very satisfying, given that in your youth, you were unable to imagine making a living from your art.

It was a bonus. No artist wants to struggle, but for some of us it can be more important to create than to eat. "Ross Penhall Incorporated" is a business that evolved from a passion. The business side of my art can hinder creativity, so I continually remind myself to "shut-up and paint." If I show up at my studio every day, everything falls into place and all is right with the world.

Now I am thinking I need to scale back; I don't need all these balls in the air. I want to keep it simple and relax more. I will always paint, but slowly over time, I plan to wean myself from the business aspect of my practice.

Part of that pressure must come from having several galleries in the U.S.

I think every artist would love to have a show in New York. It's a big stamp of approval. In the mid 90s, I told Barry Mowatt I was thinking about showing in the U.S., and he told me about the Caldwell Snyder Gallery (now Campton) in New York. In 1995, I dropped into the gallery while on vacation and spoke to the director. When I got back to Vancouver, there was a note from them asking to represent me exclusively.

As I could only be represented by one dealer, I had to make a choice and it was hard. After six years of representation, I left the Buschlen Mowatt and signed with the Caldwell Snyder in Soho, New York as well as their other locations in San Francisco and Carmel. At that time, the Canadian dollar was worth sixty cents. I was lucky. My timing was a gift. Then, in 2008, things changed.

When the recession hit?

Yes. I had a show in November 2008, and I knew what was coming. Everybody was scared about the economy. I still had steady sales, but some of my work didn't sell. The positive side of fewer sales, however, was less pressure for me to paint frenetically. It gave me more time for ideas and to travel to new landscapes. I could sketch and draw more, do some experimentation and do some printmaking at New Leaf Editions.

On another matter, it comes as a surprise to me that you advocate donating art to charities.

Barry Mowatt told me early in my career, that I needed to donate my work to certain auctions. Following his suggestion, I chose ones that felt right to me. I enjoy contributing to respectful charities of my choice. It makes me happy to know I can make a difference. I donate my best work and I hope for the best.

What message would you give emerging artists?

Sincere commitment and supportive people are prerequisites of artistic success. Success can't be measured in dollars. I would encourage artists to think about two careers: Firstly, find a vocation or a job that is rewarding and enhances your energy (as well as pays the bills) and secondly, with your enhanced zest, commit to your art everyday.

EPILOGUE

The biggest problem facing many artists is emotional decision-making in situations that demand an astute business decision. I once coached an artist who'd made so many decisions emotionally that she wound up many thousands of dollars in debt. Good business decisions are required in every career. Key decisions about your practice can ensure emotional satisfaction or artistic pride, as well as deserved financial return.

Ross' growth and success has come from making decisions based on his integrity, not his finances. As he grew as a person, he grew as an artist. Still, his change in medium was astute.

Two things remained steadfast and served his career well: His unique and appealing visual language of landscape (his creative vision) and his remarkably warm, open and honest character. Ross has a palpable joy that infuses every conversation. If you are drawn to his art and, as a result, are introduced to him, you will want to own one of his paintings. He is the quintessential nice guy.

I approached Ross because of his change in media; I was not expecting him to so comfortably bring up the subject of the "packaging" of his work, image and story. Ross is a great story—a firefighter and station captain who creates beautiful art. When there is a convergence of great art, a great story and a great personality, as with Ross, you get critical marketing mass. He is the perfect trifecta for his galleries, "the total package."

If you are lucky enough to be in his position, the most important thing to ensure, is that your ego does not inflate along with your success. Ross, in spite of being highly successful as an artist, has both feet firmly planted on the ground.

He wisely acknowledges that having lived his entire life in the same community has contributed to the development of his career. Statistics derived from a study of the practices of a few thousand B.C. artists revealed that almost 70% of their sales were to someone with whom the artist had "a relationship." Having a large social network is an extremely valuable asset for the independent artist/business person; Ross readily attracts "fans" with his engaging personality and story.

Ross' success in the U.S. market proves that, although having a network helped build his career in Vancouver, his talent is the primary reason for his success. It is impressive to note that for several years, the annual income that Ross derived from his art vastly exceeded his income derived from fire fighting.

Surprising to me was Ross' enthusiasm for charity auctions. My view had been: Why should our nation's lowest income earners support charities to the extent they do? I felt differently when the benefiting charity was a visual arts organization, but I have too often heard from artists badly treated by charity auction organizers; either receipts were not issued or issued in the wrong value, the work was sold at far too low a value, or was lost, or the buyer's contact information was not recorded. Nearly all the auction-related stories I heard were negative.

Ross, however, speaks of a vastly different experience. He was strategic in his choice of auctions. His pieces always provoked a dramatic bidding process that thrilled the audience (providing them with a rich emotional experience) and netted a sum higher than his regular gallery prices. It is clear that this strategy worked well both for the artist and for the charities with which he worked.

What will stay with me, however, is not what Ross said about the transition from drawing to oil, not the remarks about "packaging" or the public response to his work; rather, it will be his words about an inner compulsion to create. We artists are defined by our need to express, and it brings us all rich intrinsic rewards.

Ross, however, has enjoyed remarkable extrinsic rewards as well. In that regard, he is an inspiration for us all because of the other lasting impression he leaves: His grace.

LINKS

Buschlen Mowatt Gallery: www.buschlenmowatt.com
Caldwell Snyder Gallery: www.caldwellsnyder.com
Gamblin Paints: www.gamblincolors.com
Lucy Hogg: http://lucyhogg.com
Malaspina Printmakers: www.malaspinaprintmakers.com
New Leaf Editions: www.newleafeditions.com

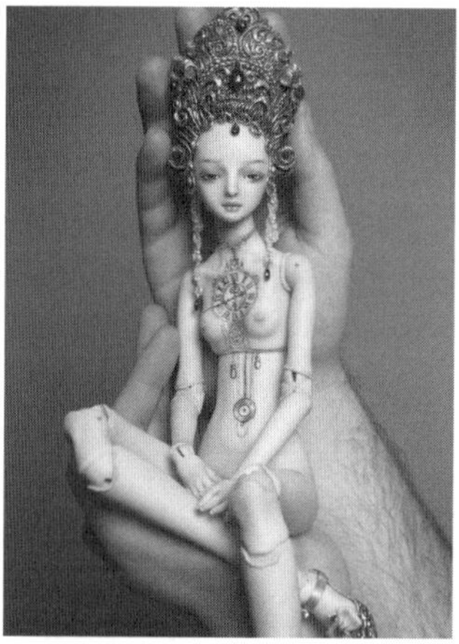

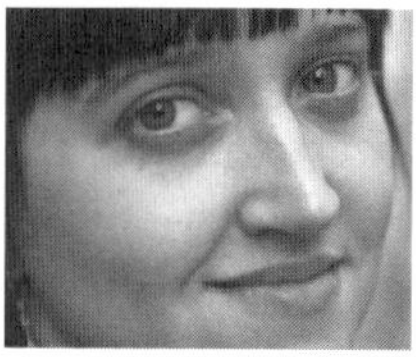

MARINA BYCHKOVA, 1982

Twenty to Midnight; porcelain, Tourmaline Rubies and bronze.
2011; 16" x 4.5" x 2.5"

www.enchanteddoll.com

12 Marina Bychkova

Marketing: Marina has combined integrity with masterful niche marketing skills to great success.

Date of interview: September 23, 2010

"When I made my first porcelain doll, I made a commitment to turn dollmaking into a career. I had done market research like a responsible person. I knew there was a market for dolls. When I made my first integrated doll, I was so happy, and I knew it was just the beginning."

— *Marina Bychkova*

PROLOGUE

Entrepreneurs are very conscious of the economics of their endeavors; artists tend to be more conscious of their process and outcomes. Entrepreneurial heaven is a monopoly on a product that fills human need; artistic products do not fulfill a need, they fulfill human desire. As vendors of products that fulfill desire, we tend to become involved in "niche marketing."

A niche market is a group of customers with a shared passion—a common desire. The ideal niche market is vast and comprised of people with significant disposable income. The ideal niche market is also characterized by easy and/or inexpensive access to its members. The artist who can develop a product that is satisfying to make and that serves the demand of a large and wealthy niche market can do very well.

When I think of Russian culture, one thing that comes to mind are the nesting dolls that fascinated me as a child. Consequently, when a friend told me about a young Russian graduate of Emily Carr University named Marina who was enjoying success making dolls, I was intrigued. I visited her website and discovered a kind of doll I had not expected and, being a guy, an art form that was not immediately engaging. But they *were* intriguing, in that every component of the body and costume was impeccably hand-made. I was very impressed with Marina's technical achievement and her sophisticated design narrative.

The global doll market has passionate aficionados who put incredible value on uniqueness; the market welcomed Marina's dolls. She sells directly to her customers, thanks to the Internet, as well as through sales intermediaries to whom she must pay a commission. Her story is of a natural passion, that, with vision, talent, training and very hard work, has led to phenomenal success in a very wealthy niche market.

Why am I writing about a maker of dolls in a book for artists? The answer is important: Because it is not the medium that is important, it is in the integrity of your process. To me, whatever is done by hand, with integrity and thoughtfulness and imbued with a compelling narrative, is art.

Marina's warm and engaging personality is a boon for her business, but ultimately her years of dedication have produced a master craftsperson who infuses her products with aesthetic sophistication. And if that weren't enough to make Marina interesting, her dolls are selling as fast as she can produce them and earning very significant prices.

I talked with Marina on the Emily Carr campus in Vancouver.

INTERVIEW

When did you first become interested in art?

I was always making things when I was little, cutting up books to make dolls. Then, as I got older, I started to draw dolls on paper and cut them out.

How old were you when you developed that interest?

I made my first doll when I was six. I lived in southwest Siberia at a time when the country was in a terrible mess. My mom enrolled me in art classes, and I had a very specific interest: I wanted to make jointed dolls. My first jointed doll had just two joints at the shoulder. I used cardboard to draw a princess, and drew her arms separately. I raided my grandpa's tool cabinet and found some nuts and bolts, and I put them through the cardboard so her arms could move.

In school, were your teachers supportive of your creativity?

We had art classes, but we were trained mostly in technical skills—applied arts— and there was an emphasis on math because the city was full of engineers. I stayed in Russia until 1997, and then my family immigrated and I enrolled in King George Secondary School in (Vancouver's) West End. When I finished there, I went on to Emily Carr University.

And did you know through high school that you would go to art school?

No. Even though I spent my childhood and adolescence making dolls—I made hundreds of them—it didn't occur to me that being creative could be a way of making a living. I always thought of it as just something to do; I never took it seriously. I felt I wasn't really good at anything. I thought I might try journalism, but I wasn't fluent in English at that point, and I didn't think I'd be able to get into UBC even though my grades were good. And then I decided to go to Emily Carr (ECU) because of my artistic inclinations.

Did you show any work you had done with dolls at Emily Carr?

I took a four-year programme in fine art at ECU, but ended up doing it over five years. I was pretty lost throughout the first two years. I had stopped making dolls because I was so traumatized by the move to Canada.

At school, the work had to be really conceptual, and dolls are so figurative—probably the most figurative thing you can think of—so my interests didn't fit with the school and I became disillusioned. I felt that everything I was making was insignificant, and that I didn't have anything to say that hadn't already been said. Every art student probably goes through this. Then it hit me like a lightning bolt at the end of my second year. I thought, "What am I doing? I love making dolls! Why haven't I made a single project?"

I decided that I would make dolls with a very strong conceptual element, otherwise my work would be viewed as craft. I took a semester off to learn how to make porcelain dolls, and the next semester I took them to school. My first ones were not like what you see today on my website, they were more rudimentary.

When I showed them at school in a critique session, it wasn't until well into the class that I said, "Well, it took me so many hours to make them." Only when I said that, did everyone realize that I had carved and molded them myself. The initial disbelief that I had made them flattered me immensely—but the dolls were hollow. They were just decorative objects. I had made everything—all the accessories, every single component of the doll—and I felt, on one hand, that I had the skills to make anything, but I realized that I had to make something with meaning. I had to make something significant.

What did that involve?

I experimented with tattooing dolls, because I was majoring in intaglio. I thought I'd apply this technique to my dolls, printing on leather. I thought I'd create a kind of leather skin and put it on the doll so it would look like a tattoo, but it didn't work. It was really difficult. Then I started my breakthrough project which was a series called *The Comfort of Conformity*.

It was while I was in third year at Emily Carr. I drew hybrid clothes, restrictive fashion items such as a straightjackets and orthopaedic corsets, as fashion. I printed them on fabric and put them on androgynous dolls with baby faces. They were very asexual, yet, at the same time, they were sexualized through the restrictive clothing. I took the work to several crit sessions and it was received better than my previous dolls that were merely decorative. They stirred thought in my classmates and my teachers. Then I started engraving porcelain freehand, with a sewing needle. I wouldn't be in the place I am now, creatively or conceptually, without my training at Emily Carr. It has contributed significantly to my development as an artist.

Did you continue to work with dolls in year final years of schooling?

Yes. My grad project was two ball-jointed porcelain dolls based on the tale of *Snow White and the Seven Dwarfs*.

How did you create these ball-joints, these articulations?

I sculpted all the parts. I worked out dimensions and had to engineer the sockets for movement, but it's not very advanced mechanics. From the very moment I started them, I knew I wanted to make dolls that balanced form and function; most dolls are only one or the other. All the dolls I saw were either fragile, pretty figurines that couldn't be touched, or they were kiddie dolls for kids to destroy. I wanted to make something for adults; porcelain is not child-friendly.

Are the joints made of porcelain as well?

Yes. The entire doll is made of porcelain. The joints are lined with leather, so that when the porcelain moves, it doesn't grate against itself. Inside the doll there's a custom carbon-steel spring strung with industrial-grade wire.

And why do you like porcelain?

I like it because of its incredible resilience to the elements. It's impervious and very tough. It emulates skin nicely because it has a nice transparency, and when you polish it, it becomes smooth as silk. What compelled me to make porcelain dolls was when I watched a special on the Titanic on the Discovery Channel. They showed a doll face lying on the bottom of the ocean; it was lying in the dirt, and the image of it was so haunting. For eighty years, it had been there, and so I knew it was the material I wanted to work with.

What happened after graduation?

When I made my first porcelain doll, I made a commitment to turn doll making into a career. I had done market research like a responsible person, so I knew there was a market for dolls. When I made my first integrated doll, I was so happy, and I knew it was just the beginning. I could see it all in my head. But first I had to repay my student loans. I had six months to repay my loans without interest, so I worked retail and made dolls on the side. I worked almost 24/7. I slept for only a couple hours a night. I worked eight hours at the store, and I'd come home and put another eight hours into dolls, building up inventory because my fiancé decided he was going to make me a website. I made it my goal to repay all $15,000 of my loan without paying interest and, as I was living with my parents, I was able to do it.

One day I was carrying wood from the hardware store, and a guy volunteered to help me carry all my stuff. We started talking on the way back, and I told him I was making a stand for my dolls and that I made dolls, and then, as we parted, he gave me his card and said, "I'm a journalist and I'd like to interview you about your work. It sounds really interesting." And then I got my first sale. Everything happened all at once.

Was it a local sale?

No, it was from England. And then I sold one to someone from Moscow, and things started snowballing. Without any advertising—just the website.

And were most of your sales international?

I have only sold one doll to a Canadian resident.

How did you handle sales?

Customers had to use PayPal or direct deposit into my bank. For the first couple years I was wearing several hats. I wasn't just an artist who created merchandise, I also had to sell it. Customers would write me and place an order, and then I would schedule their project and give them a delivery date.

Were your dolls always very elaborate and time consuming to make?

I had a small inventory of costumed dolls that I started selling, but then my dad had this idea that I should make a naked doll to sell. Instead of spending four hundred hours on a costumed doll, he thought I should produce a naked doll in a week. So I thought I'd try it, even though I wasn't crazy about the idea. But they started selling, and within months there was a huge demand for nude porcelain dolls. So that's how it went on for a year or two—selling lots of nude dolls and some costumed dolls—and then I felt secure enough and that I had enough orders to quit my retail job.

I worked alone for a while, and then my fiancé lost his job. He had already been helping me with my website, so we just decided that he would work with me. He started by helping me around the studio, handling sales and more of the business issues, but he has actually started making dolls. Now both of us are so busy that we need another person!

How long has your business been supporting the two of you?

For two years now, and I never expected that this would happen. I was expecting hardship. But my parents have encouraged me—my dad, particularly, has always told me that I could do anything. I grew up with this attitude of, "Yes, I can."

What's the Louis Vuitton story?

A couple years ago I was in Paris at a show, and I met Fabrizio Viti who is the head shoe designer for Louis Vuitton, a very well established fashion house in Paris, and we became friends. Obviously he's a very well connected person, and he's exposed my work to people in high places.

He taught me about high-end couture fashion. I was never a fashionista; I was never into labels. But after I had met him, I became more familiar with the world of high fashion and realized it's a form of art in itself. I started bringing a couture sensibility into my work, adding extravagance and an element of avant garde.

And you started selling on eBay?

I sold a couple of dolls on eBay. I put them there just for fun, to see what people would bid on a doll. I started at $2,000 I think, but my first doll sold for $8,000! And the second doll sold for $14,000 and it just went from there.

How can you list a doll at $2,000 on your website when you're getting thousands more on eBay?

For a while, it was a huge conflict and I didn't know what to do. When this happened, I had a year's worth of orders and the deposits had been paid. I couldn't raise the prices and had to stick with my commitments.

But you could put more work on eBay?

I could have, but I had a solo show in Berlin. I had fourteen dolls in it, in the range of $6,000 - $35,000 US, and twelve of them sold right away. The others sold shortly thereafter.

So, basically, you can sell everything you make!

Exactly. I never have any inventory. But when I sell directly, I earn the full retail price. When someone sells for me, like the gallery in Germany, I have to pay a commission.

So why would you use a gallery?

Galleries are established venues. There's still prestige that goes with showing in a gallery. It validates me as an artist, and it exposes me to an altogether different clientele.

How did you choose the gallery in Germany?

They chose me. They asked me for a couple of dolls that sold right away, so they asked for more dolls, and now we've been working together for over two years.

I don't show in galleries very much. It's too labour intensive. My dolls are becoming more popular; they've been featured in lots of pop culture publications. One of my dolls was on the cover of a magazine wearing a custom made Louis Vuitton dress made for the photo shoot. I think I've been featured in close to eighty publications in the last couple of years. I never imagined this could happen to me.

EPILOGUE

Okay, we can't all create objects that sell for tens of thousands of dollars on eBay, but what we can learn from Marina is the value of (pragmatic) intuition, to trust our own instincts and to stay true to our passions. This is an approach to work that many artists share with Marina. What she did, however, was market research. She was practical in her approach; she knew that there was a market—a rich market—for dolls, and she knew that her dolls were different than the others offered in the marketplace. And this is something we can all do. The Internet makes the entire world available to us; we can serve a market that may be small where we live, but large enough globally, to support us.

Niche marketing is widely practiced by visual artists: Think of all the artists who do western-style art, or wildlife, botanicals abstracts, surrealism or boats. But a new twist to niche marketing is the nature of nomenclature—"tags" on Etsy or keywords on other sites—that serve as search parameters on web search engines. These descriptors serve visitors to aggregate sites to help them find the items they seek; keywords or tags serve niche buyers.

Every adjective you use to describe your work helps to determine and locate its market, whether online or in the real world. Consider all your descriptors carefully and consult with objective voices; sometimes they see things in your work that you cannot.

LINKS

eBay: www.cafr.ebay.ca
PayPal: www.paypal.ca/ca
Louis Vuitton: www.louisvuitton.com

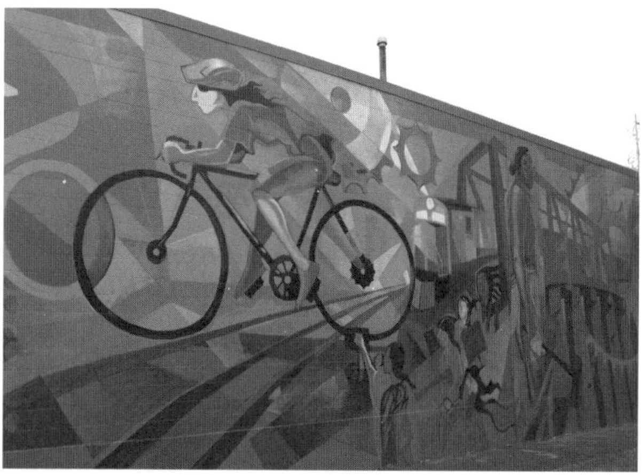

Photos by Esther Rausenberg

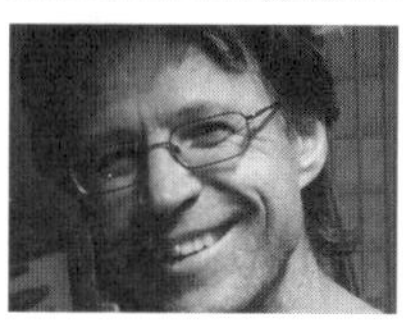

RICHARD TETRAULT, 1951

Mural, Adanac Street, Vancouver, BC
Eastside Mural Projects; 2009
Artistic Director: R. Tetrault

http://richard-tetrault.ca

13 Richard Tetrault

Integration: Richard's involvement with public art has enhanced his community and his career.

Date of interview: October 19, 2010

"I like community engagement. What I create comes from the community. That is really exciting to me... Working with artists from varied artistic and cultural backgrounds is profoundly valuable to me. I believe it is a worthy catalyst for change within our community."

— *Richard Tetrault*

PROLOGUE

The question I am asked most often is: "How can I get a gallery to represent me?" The best answer that I have ever heard to this question is to get fully involved with your local community and in the operations of the galleries that interest you. Besides furthering your potential for representation, however, creative involvement with your community has many other professional benefits for artists. And perhaps there is no better way for you to become involved with your community than through the creation of public art.

Public art can take many forms. It can be winning a commission for the installation of an artwork in a public space, or it can be an outcome of an artist-in-residence program. But the methodology I admire most, is for artists to invest themselves in their community in accordance with a public art philosophy called "community cultural development" or CCD.

CCD is a practice well known to many arts and community leaders. It is a movement that advocates the involvement of artists in community dialogue, and whereas the CCD philosophy is becoming better known in Canadian communities, many artists have been involved in the practice for a long time. A key principal of a CCD project is that the artists are consultative, focusing more on the *process* of the community dialogue; leadership in the determination of project objectives rests with the community. CCD projects partner artists with community leaders and they involve community members in a creative process designed to produce outcomes that enhance the quality of life in the host community.

CCD projects have budgets that, in the hands of clever community leaders, can provoke funding from sources normally unavailable to artists. As well, artists involved with CCD projects can sometimes add to a project budget from traditional arts funding sources, and the combined resources can facilitate major community projects. The benefit to the community is obvious; less measurable are the intrinsic rewards that come to the active participants of CCD projects.

Significant benefits can accrue to you if you initiate, or become part of, a CCD project in your community. I must stress, however, that the beneficial professional outcomes an artist can enjoy from involvement with a CCD project are by-products of involvement; artists do not undertake their projects in order to achieve these outcomes.

To use business vocabulary, one practical value of involvement with a CCD project in your community, is the benefit of increased "brand awareness." Far more people will know your name and that you are an artist at the end of a successful CCD project; the bigger the project and the more people involved, the better.

Involvement with a public art project often means that your name will pass before many eyes and through many civic minds as your project is developed. As you raise funds, obtain permits and partnerships, and as you involve the media in your project, people not only meet you, they meet you in the context of a highly creative and socially concerned initiative. At the end of the exercise, many school teachers and school board officials, a huge number of students and their parents, community activists, bureaucrats, park board officials and/or religious leaders will know who you are and about the work you do. Consequently, whenever any one of them might need creative services, your name may come to mind.

The execution of public art projects can dramatically enhance your professional presentation in your portfolio, website and CV. As well, CCD experience can also serve well to illustrate that you have the respect and support of your community on grant and residency applications. And whereas it can be extremely hard for an individual artist to earn the attention of the media, the artist at the centre of a CCD project can often access media because there is a far larger constituency of interest in a story about a beneficial community project, than in an individual.

Having lived and worked in Vancouver all my life, and as a cultural worker particularly focused on the visual arts, I cannot remember when I first heard about, and met, Richard Tetrault. He is the consummate artist/community animator. As a founding member of the Eastside Culture Crawl, an Artist-in-Residence of the Vancouver Board of Parks and Recreation, and as a leader in public art mural making, Richard is fully engaged in his community.

I wanted to talk to Richard because of his involvement with CCD long before the term and philosophy emerged. I interviewed him in his Strathcona studio.

INTERVIEW

When did you first become aware of an interest in the visual arts?

Watching my mom paint when I grew up in White Rock. She was a self-taught painter, actor, and singer, and she was very involved with arts and culture. And my dad was self-taught in music, so I'd say that my parents were my inspiration. I remember watching my mom paint when I was five years old and trying to copy her, and I remember feeling exasperated because I couldn't copy her as well as I thought I should.

Did you study art in school?

Oh, definitely. And my mom enrolled me in a summer outdoor painting class in White Rock that I totally took to. In fact, I'm sure some of my best paintings were done back then, and it's been catch-up ever since. By high school, I was painting several hours a day, skipping out of as many classes as I could. Fortunately, I had some good art teachers who really supported my way of learning.

And then, when you finished high school, what happened?

While I was in high school, I was going to the Vancouver School of Art classes for teens on Saturdays. I studied with Gordon Payne, who was a really profound influence. He gave me an enthusiasm for creativity—he and Egbert Oudendag. Egbert was a Dutch self-taught artist who lived in a beautiful place on the shore in White Rock. He really believed in making money from his art. He was living a good life supported by his painting and I thought, "Well this looks like a really good lifestyle!"

Were you exhibiting at this time?

My first show was at our house in White Rock when I was sixteen, and it was pretty successful. By the time I was eighteen, I was showing at a couple of galleries in Vancouver and White Rock, so I was exhibiting pretty early on.

And after graduation, did you go to the Vancouver School of Art?

No. I wanted to go to university because I thought it would be an important experience, and I enrolled in music. At the same time, I was studying visual art on my own and getting my teacher's certificate in music through the

Royal Conservatory. But I got restless and hit the road. I went up north to work, and then I went travelling to Africa. That was the 70s; it was kind of a "dream time" for people with restless feet. I went all over the place, and in the mid seventies I started going to Mexico. That is how I got into murals; I really profoundly connected with them.

I wanted to find things out on my own. I might have learned things quicker had I stayed in school, but it didn't suit my temperament. I moved to the Gulf Islands for a while, taught myself printmaking, traveled to New York to study figure drawing and anatomy at the Art Students League, and I also kept returning to Mexico for more exposure to the murals. I began to understand their language, and I think they've influenced me as much as anything I've seen in Canadian, American and European work. There's something about them really that struck a cord with me.

Obviously, when I was in Europe, I visited museums like the Louvre and the Prado, and I was amazed by what I saw. I didn't go to Rome, so maybe had I seen Michelangelo, I would have been inspired by the Renaissance, but the whole socio-political facet of the Mexican culture and their murals doesn't exist in Italian work. Murals were the voice of the downtrodden for people who couldn't read, and they celebrate the history of the indigenous people, They are fascinating to me.

In the United States, there has been a popular movement of mural making, evolving from Mexican, Chicano and Afro-American communities; they have been a vehicle for expression, empowerment and collaboration. A myriad of artists from various backgrounds have created ambitious, symbolically charged, and beautifully executed murals in cities across the States. These too have been influential for me.

Did you set up a studio in Vancouver?

A critical event in my career was moving into a derelict old Vancouver building on Powell Street near Oppenheimer Park. It was on the fringe of what was then called "Japantown," in the heart of the Vancouver's Downtown Eastside; it was a really amazing eye-opener for me.

Initially, I went there because it was affordable. We got a whole floor of a building for $100 a month and turned it into a very funky studio. It was the beginning of building a community of like-minded artists who really wanted to work at their art. We wanted to work hard and have a cheap place to do it. I realized that it takes a lot of time to really learn your craft, and you need the luxury of time. You either have to get a job to make money, or you have to learn to live for next to nothing to have enough time to create. And then, once we moved in to the studio, I realized that the Downtown Eastside was, and remains, a really profoundly rich community.

How were you selling your work at this time?

I let go of my galleries because it was the 80s and a hard time to sell art. I would do shows, but very often they were in parallel spaces. I wasn't focused on sales. Then, because I wanted to go to Mexico, I opened my studio up and advertised it amongst a circle of people who I knew were interested in my work. I sold a lot and thought to myself, "Hey, that was really good! I cleared out some space and I can go to Mexico." That made me realize how much people love coming into an artist's studio where there's this energy of production and creativity.

Was that experience the beginning of the Eastside Culture Crawl?

The Crawl came about after we got this building in 1993. At that time, there were four groups of us sharing it. It was a bit of a fix-up job, and the neighbourhood was very curious about what we were doing, so we decided to have an open house. That was in 1993.

We did a display about a couple of community issues at that time, and tied it in with an auction/ fundraiser to raise money for the people who had been arrested protesting the logging of Clayoquot Sound. After that, we did some AIDS fundraising for a few people we knew who needed medications, and then we raised funds for neighbours whose house had burnt down. Every year it was a different issue, but the main thing was this idea of an open studio and somehow serving the community.

The second year we all combined our mailing lists so we would get a big crowd, then we became aware that Parker Street and Williams Street studios were doing something similar around the same time of year. I remember having a meeting over at Parker Street with a handful of people representing different buildings and different studios, when we decided to combine our dates.

Then we were three buildings, but even Parker Street didn't have that many artists participating because it was such a new concept. And each year it expanded. It went from maybe thirty or forty artists when we united, to the (almost) four hundred artists and close to fifty buildings we have now. Even if you're not a commercial artist, or if you're an installation artist, where else are you going to get a few thousand people seeing your work in one weekend!

And when an artist is shy—and a lot of artists are—the Crawl kind of forces you to think and speak about your work. Artists realize, after a few years, that if they do a really well put-together exhibit, they get a better response. They learn that if they really take care, clear up the clutter and put their best work out, people will come back the next year. Artist Wendy D., from the ARC building, is now doing professional development workshops for artists on how to prepare for the Crawl.

Do you know how many people are attracted to the event?

Tens of thousands, I'm sure. We have two-to-three thousand people through our space alone. The Crawl is such a great tool. It really is like a movement that developed organically. For so many years it was totally ad-hoc, but eventually we formed a board of directors and became a not-for-profit society. I am involved with an affiliate program called Studio 101 that brings students from local schools into the studios after the Crawl is over for a special afternoon. All the kids—and most of them have never been in a studio—get workshops.

Besides the Crawl, you've been involved in other ways with the Downtown Eastside, right?

In 1980 I was asked to start teaching drawing at the Carnegie Centre. It opened in 1980 as a living room for people on the Downtown Eastside, and it was kind of a home base for me. It has a kitchen, cheap food, a library, and it has a great sense of community. I set up portrait drawing classes that ran for eight years, about fifty weeks a year. I'd bribe models from the Centre with coffee and that really influenced me because anybody who sits in a chair long enough, starts telling you their story.

And in drawing the life of the Downtown Eastside, you found inspiration for creating murals?

I did. In the mid-80s, I initiated a few things, collaborating with Public Dreams Society on some public installations. We worked with the community, using art as a way to profile community issues such as traffic programs and community gardens. I got different artists in the community to make a guardian spirit to mount on a pole in front of the community gardens, for example. Our work would provide the media with the visuals they needed to draw attention to the threatened spaces.

But the first mural I did was for Simon Fraser University Student Union. That was my first really big mural commission. Then I started dropping off my CV with a proposal about mural painting at a few schools, and I got a tremendous response.

And the Vancouver School Board paid you?

At first the schools were paying me, but the School Board had an Artists-in-Residence Programme and I got onto their list of artists. I did that for almost twenty years. I developed a whole programme about designing murals from the ground up. It wasn't me doing the design and then the students coming along and painting it, we did the research together and it was *they* who had to come up with the ideas and the scale drawings. The mural had to be about a theme that they believed in. Eventually, I combined printmaking and mural painting; it is something that I still do through the UBC Education Department. I also got involved with the ArtStarts in the Schools program; I have done a lot of workshops with them. And, my mural work has led to work with a Canada-wide coalition called La Raza Group. We've been doing projects over the last several years in Argentina, Mexico, Cuba and different parts of Canada.

I'm hearing that your practice involves a lot of time teaching and doing community work.

I'm in the studio maybe half of the year; otherwise, I'm out doing projects.

And you earn income from your project sponsors and when you are hired as a teacher?

Yes. And, of course, you have to raise money and write grants and all that stuff. But a great resource and support for me has been my partner, Esther

Rausenberg. She works part-time, and her employment income has allowed us to do what we do. We've formed a non-profit society to do public art and she's really involved in our international projects.

It seems to me that when you moved to Strathcona, Vancouver's Downtown Eastside, got a seriously committed artist-in-residence for life.

I like community engagement. What I create comes from the community. That is really exciting to me. Working with the Aboriginal community on Hastings Street was really profound, for example. Doing that huge mural on the reconditioned Orwell Hotel on Hastings Street served many purposes. It showcases a renewed Native social housing development, and it also serves to advertise that there's a gallery on the main floor. It is a new gallery, showing urban Aboriginal artists. Working with artists from varied artistic and cultural backgrounds is profoundly valuable to me. I believe it is a worthy catalyst for change within our community.

EPILOGUE

Communities, amenities and creators benefit when artists undertake public art installations, community artist residencies and when artists undertake Community Cultural Development (CCD) projects. Richard's community involvement reflects his love of Mexican muralists and their social, as well as aesthetic, ambitions.

The way you get involved with public art in your community will very different. The point is, no matter how you participate, getting involved with your community can open doors to further opportunities.

If you cannot involve yourself in public art in a way that earns you money, nothing beats volunteering as a way of earning the respect and recognition of your peers. And active, thoughtful volunteering can create some of the same benefits that accrue to artists who win (funded) public art commissions. As artists, we have creative thinking skills, design skills, passion and energy to offer our communities, and the more extensive and diverse our volunteer services, the better for our career and our community's wellbeing. Richard's work enriches his spirit, the spirits of those with whom he works and the spirits of the community members who enjoy his project outcomes.

How do you find out about public art opportunities in your community? You do your research. Use the Internet. I Googled "public art in Canada," and "public art programs + [city name] " and found lots of information. Plus, each site I visited had links to other aggregate resource sites. Cities, schools, community centres, arts councils, churches, business associations or chambers of commerce, park boards, hospitals, prisons, care facilities, large commercial projects: All the agencies of our social infrastructure are potential partners for enterprising artists interested in public art.

The successful procurement of public art commissions is a similar process to the procurement of a commission or sale. It takes imagination, networking and the development of a strong creative brand for yourself. Successfully winning a public art competition also requires healthy administrative, bookkeeping, fundraising and writing skills. The effort, however, is powerfully worthwhile.

Getting your first public art project is the hardest; the more you do, the easier the opportunities are to secure. A good way to get started, is to talk to artists with experience and/or to partner with experienced artists in a public art proposal.

LINKS

ArtStarts in the Schools: http://artstarts.com
Art Students' League: www.theartstudentsleague.org
East Side Culture Crawl: www.eastsideculturecrawl.com
La Raza Group: www.larazagroup.com
Public Dreams Society: http://publicdreams.org
Wendy D: http://wendyd.com

For information about the Parker Street and William Street studios, the Artist Resource Centre (ARC) and other artist studio collectives, please visit the Eastside Culture Crawl address and click on "Buildings."

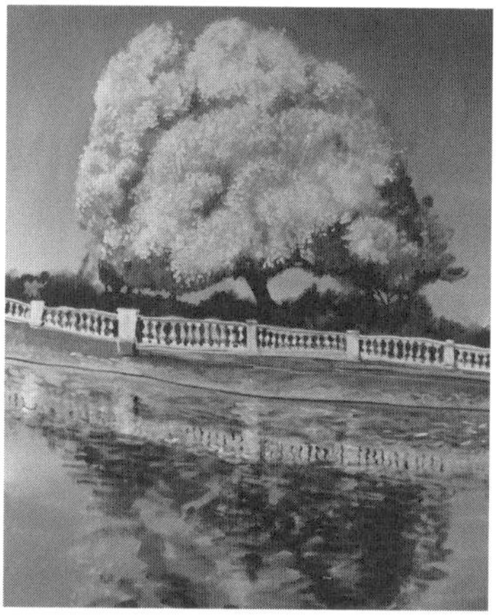

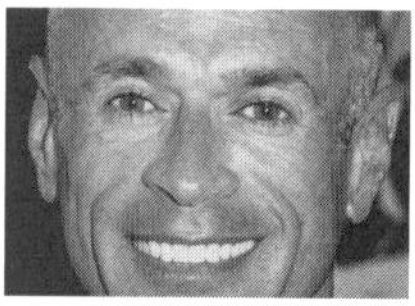

TIKO KERR, 1953
The Lazarus Tree; acrylic on canvas
2008; 96" x 72"

www.tikokerr.com

14 Tiko Kerr

Narrative: Tiko dramatically advanced his career by turning adversity into triumph.

Date of interview: September 23, 2010

"It was a profound experience getting so positive a response to my work. It was totally humbling, and I felt that I was brought back for a reason. I wanted to honour the people that saved my life, so I'm using my art more for social justice and celebrating my community."

— *Tiko Kerr*

PROLOGUE

For emotional impact, nothing beats the uplifting story of Tiko Kerr, the human being, and Tiko Kerr, the artist. The climax of both narratives was his recent fight for life that involved a desperate quest for government permission to obtain and take unapproved medications.

The emotional consequence of adversity is often a powerful motivator for artists, but when the narrative of an artwork is of loss, grief and/or anger, such work can have a hard time finding a market. In general, customers want work with positive connotations. It is my experience that the narrative of a work is an important part of the customer's consideration when buying art, and a sad narrative can be far less motivating.

A crisis can have unexpected consequences. How we respond to one is a measure of our worth, and our response can shape some of our resultant outcomes. One of Tiko's responses to the catastrophic turn of events in his battle with disease, was to paint. That is not surprising for an artist, but his crisis heightened his senses. His exhibition, *The Lazarus Tree*, took his work to new critical heights. His narrative was about triumph. And in a dramatic surge of creative experiment, painting on his medication bottles, he created a powerful and redemptive image that moved from the personal to the universal.

I talked with Tiko in his studio.

INTERVIEW

When did you first become aware of your interest in the visual arts?

I grew up as an only child and spent a lot of time drawing. I developed pretty good skills, but I went all the way through school pursuing science, which I loved.

You didn't study art?

I did take art classes, but art wasn't much more than fun for me. I was often getting drawing awards at the end of the academic year, but it didn't occur to me that art was actually something of value. Then, after I got my undergraduate degree in biology, I decided to go backpacking for a few months and wound up going around the world twice, over a period of five-and-a-half years. The whole time, I did sketchbooks; I filled them with drawings and paintings and sent them home. Then, when I came back to Calgary, an artist friend said, "Why don't we have a two man show?" I said fine, and everything sold. After that, I just kind of continued on my way and forgot about going back to school.

Did the sales make you commit to being an artist?

The adventures I had on my trip pretty much stripped me of my old personality. I explored my sexuality and had a couple of near-death experiences; all kinds of things that happened made my previous life seem less relevant. And I learned, on the road, about how to incorporate everything that comes into your life into what you do. I had the audacity of a twenty-year-old that convinced me that I was just going to keep going forward in a very adventurous way.

Did you get a job, or were you able to earn all your income as an artist?

I had obtained Australian residency when I was on the road, and I had to go back and forth between Canada and Australia to maintain my dual status. I was trying to set up a studio in two places—Vancouver and Sydney. I would work odd jobs during the day, and paint at night. And then I met Craig, my partner, twenty-six years ago. He's been generous enough to allow me to paint full time. Frankly don't know how other artists do it without someone's support. I was lucky. We gave up our Australian residency in 1986 and moved back to Canada; it was too difficult to maintain two houses and travel back and forth. I kept having to start all over again every time we moved, so we came back full of piss and vinegar, and I painted furiously. I walked into Buschlen Mowatt Gallery one day and said, "You don't know me, but I think you should show my work." And they agreed. I had my first professional exhibition there in 1988. Being on the road taught me to just go for it.

And what was the subject material of your paintings then?

My first exhibition at Buschlen Mowatt was a series of empty deck chairs. I thought it was just about something outside my window, but looking back, it's very autobiographical. It's a consideration of loss and what we are all going to be facing. At that time, I had just discovered that I was HIV positive. That was actually the reason that we moved back to Canada. I wanted to be closer to my family because, in those days, there was no hope. It was basically a death sentence. The doctor told me to go home and put my affairs in order.

I thought that throughout my career, I was keeping my HIV status disguised. I didn't want people to feel sorry for me; I wanted the focus to be on my work. I thought there was no evidence of my secret in my work, but it's interesting now, looking back, to see that it runs all the way through it. I do a PowerPoint presentation sometimes, and I show twenty-five years of my work. I can show what the work looked like when I was feeling good and, conversely, how my work changed in its intensity and colour when I was feeling bad.

Did all your income come from gallery sales or did you have other sources of income?

I was really lucky. I painted quickly. I think that to be successful as an artist means you really have to be able to produce a lot of work. My work just kept selling and selling.

Through Buschlen Mowatt?

Yes, but for a while I also had a gallery in Palm Springs and they couldn't keep my work in stock. It just kept selling, and I was naive enough to think that it would go on forever.

Are you still with Buschlen Mowatt?

I was with them for three years, and then I went to Dianne Farris Gallery for three years. After that, I took a break from dealers for about four years. Then I had a great relationship, for seven years, with the Heffel Gallery. They believed that the more my work was seen, the better. I think that is a very healthy attitude. So I sold out of my studio *and* I sold with them. They also gave me the opportunity to show in their auctions, but then their auctions became so profitable that they understandably became their chief focus. They regretted that they couldn't give me a show every year, and so we parted on very good terms.

Later, I had a dealer in Toronto, but my output was fluctuating so I wasn't eager to break into other markets. Instead, I focused on what was really engaging me, which is Vancouver. I became more of a regional artist, and that has really worked well for me.

Was this when you started painting Vancouver landscapes?

I painted scenes of Vancouver when I first arrived in the late 70s. I suppose I have just gotten deeper into knowing the subject, and because Vancouverites are so passionate about their city, my work sells really well. There is an infinite resource for me in the subject material and I cannot keep up to the demand for images that have something to do with Vancouver.

And do you donate to charity auctions?

Yes, I've been doing that for twenty years. I got started through Buschlen Mowatt and Jacqui Cohen's *Face the World* galas, and *Splash* for Arts Umbrella.

Were you careful about which auctions you supported?

Yes, and I refused silent auctions because I'd been burned doing them. I only donate to live auctions. But there are too many auctions now and the market can't support them. Things have slowed down somewhat, so I won't participate if I feel my work will not achieve its market value or if the organizers are inexperienced. It's really important to me to protect the value of my work.

However, if I feel strongly about supporting a not-for-profit organization, I'll join the board of directors or do collaborations. I have this kind of relationship with about half a dozen charities. I did three collaborations with a ballet company, for example.

How did that work?

I painted on stage with Ballet British Columbia. And then we worked on a three-year-long project, a Canadian ballet called *Boy Wonder*. I designed the environment.

Besides being satisfying, these collaborations put your work and name in front of a large audience, I assume.

They do. And like the charity work, it can only enhance your reputation. My main focus, however, is still my commitment to making work that has resonance. In spite of it all, I was getting no critical attention whatsoever for my work. I wasn't sure if it was because I was doing things like the Sun

Run imagery, or what, but I wondered if maybe my work was considered kind of soft. The postmodernism that is happening in conceptual art, and which Vancouver is all about, is just not the way I work. I don't get an idea and then explore a clever way to express it; I just react to things in a very visceral way. I try not to direct things too much.

Are you still with a gallery?

I was with the Windsor Gallery for a few exhibitions, but I gave that up. I don't think there's ever been a better time for artists to show their work globally through the Internet. I think the relationship of artist and gallery needs to be redefined. The gallery should not have the right to access any sales that you can generate through your own site on the Internet.

I've reached a place where I'm healthy again, I've got my strength back and I'm painting. I'm really at the height of my creative powers, and I've got a reputation. People support me, and they like my work, so now I'm pretty much done with galleries. But that may change.

You mentioned a lack of critical response to your work. But "The Lazarus Tree" exhibition brought you the critical response you were seeking, did it not?

It did. It was a profound experience getting so positive a response to my work. It was totally humbling, and I felt that I was brought back for a reason. I wanted to honour the people that saved my life, so I'm using my art more for social justice and celebrating my community.

When you have to fight for your life like I had to do, and you win, you tap into a life force that is indomitable. And that's what I'm still enjoying. Don't f--k with anyone who's had to fight for his life and won, because he will never give up. I've discovered that power and I think that force was evident in my *Lazarus Tree* exhibition.

It's a privilege to be an artist, to come to the studio every day and do what I do. My responsibility is to share that life experience, that energy, that spirituality, in my work. That's what I take very seriously. The subject matter doesn't matter. It's the application of the colour and the paint and all that.

EPILOGUE

We are all the product of our accumulated experience. Tiko's long-sought critical acclaim came to him in response to his *Lazarus Tree* exhibition and, in particular, to his self–portraits, but the works in that show were the culmination of decades of experience. By sticking to his quest, he finally fully achieved his goal, his journey assisted by his partner, Craig, and his victory inspired by his fight for life. The importance of tenacity is one lesson of his story.

This is what I took from Tiko's story:

1. He is in a long-term relationship and his partner, who supports his commitment to an artistic profession, provides a stable emotional in which Tiko can work. And, as he says, most artists need diverse sources of income and/or support.
2. He has a confident personality, which is a very valuable asset to an independent creative business person. He responds vibrantly to any interest—personal, media or corporate—in his career. Beyond that, he is entrepreneurial.
3. He produces work to his own standards that is marketable. And he is productive. He can deliver the inventory a thriving practice requires.
4. He has achieved a satisfying critical response to his work.

Regarding point number one: Not all of us can afford to be artists all the time. Sometimes we have to be employees. Sometimes, however, we enjoy the support of a partner. Many artists, and a lot of great artists, have benefited enormously from the financial and emotional support of not just partners, but of whole families. We would not know the work of Vincent van Gogh as we do today, were it not for the love of his brother, Théo, and Théo's wife Johanna van Gogh-Bonger.

Regarding point number two: Tiko is a confident and entrepreneurial person. He is also smart. These characteristics are shared by many of the most successful artists. I tend to discount "luck" as a factor of success, but our personality and our relationship to risk are factors over which we have little control—so success can certainly involve a level of luck.

Tiko is "lucky," therefore, to have a personality that accommodates complete openness about his life, a capacity that brings undeniable benefit to his artistic business. If you want to achieve significant success in the visual arts but lack his extroversion, or if you are not strong in self-advocacy, you must consider a compensatory strategy that may involve professional training, collective initiative and/or the hiring of professional services.

Another element of luck for Tiko is his gender. Statistically, although far more women self-identify as artists than men, the work of the notorious feminist art collective, the Gorilla Girls, reveals the extent to which males dominate the boards of directors and exhibition schedules of public galleries, and that males are, by far, the highest income-earners in the visual arts all over the world.

Regarding point number three: Tiko is doing brisk business creating recognizable images of Vancouver for a prideful civic population. I applaud the pragmatic management of his artistic practice; it is an approach to career management that does not intrude on his capacity to retain creative integrity.

I am often in the presence of artists who believe the market must come to them on their terms. Their opposite is, of course, those artists who sometimes are labelled as "sell outs" or "commercial." The truth is, it is hard to be an artist, and a balanced practice often involves a mix of completely speculative work with work developed with the market in mind. Tiko, do not forget, has enjoyed spousal financial support. Without it, his approach to his practice might be quite different. Artists who are solely reliant on sales for the entirety of their income must be, to some degree, either very pragmatic and/or highly entrepreneurial.

Perhaps what strikes me most in Tiko's story is his move to direct sales and away from (commissioned) gallery sales. For many of my students, representation is the dominant desire, but Tiko, like other artists in this book, makes us think about the emotional and financial cost of representation. As he says, with today's global market so readily available via the Internet, being represented by a gallery is something every artist should consider carefully.

Regarding point number four: The point of interviewing Tiko was to discuss his experience with *The Lazarus Tree* exhibition. When the narrative of your work is compelling and invokes the emotions of your audience, magic happens. And what is more emotional and compelling than a victorious, and incredibly public, hard-fought battle for life? Over-the-top life-altering experiences test our mettle; sometimes they define us. They are portals to change. We rise or fall with our reaction to them. Tiko spoke of the determination of the survivor. His fight not only saved his life, it brought him the critical satisfaction we all seek for our work.

LINKS

Ballet British Columbia: www.balletbc.com
Buschlen Mowatt Gallery: www.buschlenmowatt.com
Windsor gallery: www.winsorgallery.com

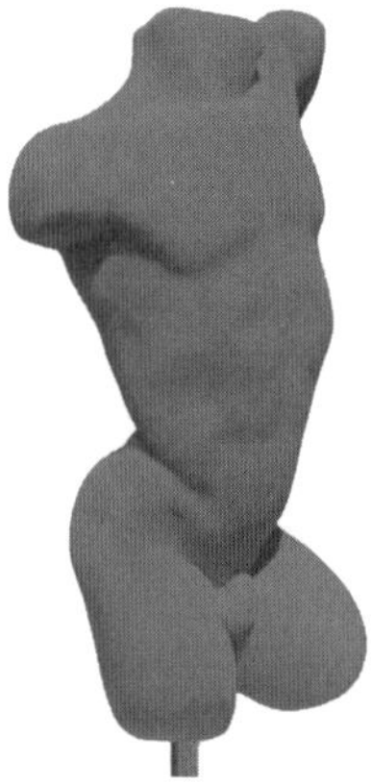

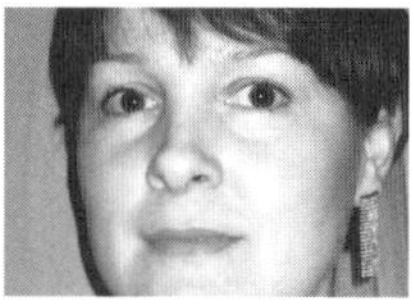

KITTY BLANDY, 1966

Red Torso; flocked cast plastic
2002; Approx. 15" x 6" x 6"

http://kittyblandy.com

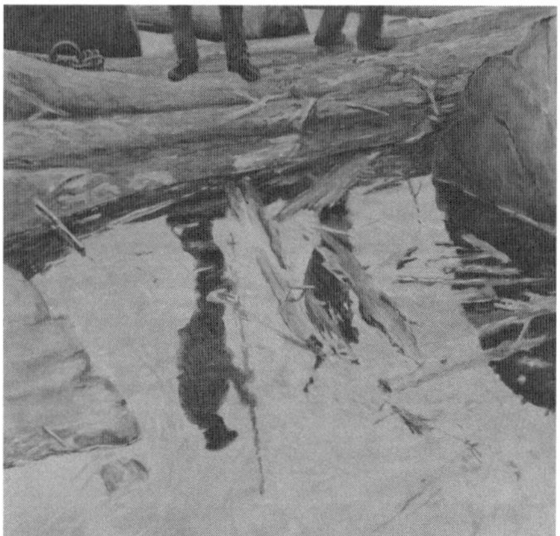

Photo by J. Fulton

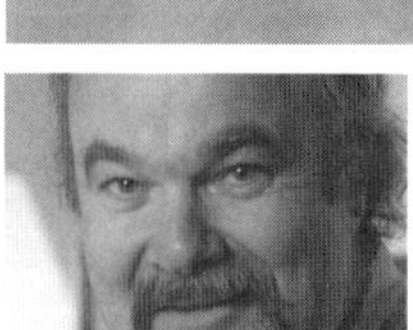

MARCUS BOWCOTT, 1951

Reflection; oil on canvas
2008; 36" x 36"

www.marcusbowcott.com

15 Gallery Representation

Kitty Blandy, Marcus Bowcott, Tiko Kerr and Val Nelson discuss gallery representation.

Date of interview: January 24, 2011

"Young emerging artists, just starting to see where they fit, shouldn't send a submission to galleries without doing their homework. Does the gallery pay their artists? Do they offer solo shows? Talk to artists who are showing in the galleries that interest you and make sure that you know what you're getting into. Also, just going into the gallery and talking to staff can give you a sense of what it would mean to do business with them."

— *Val Nelson*

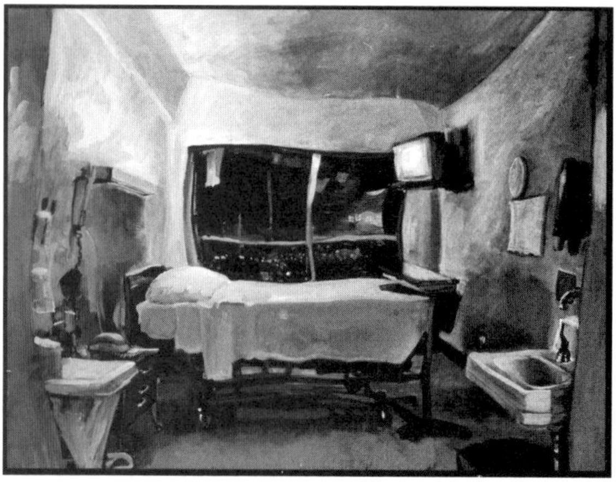

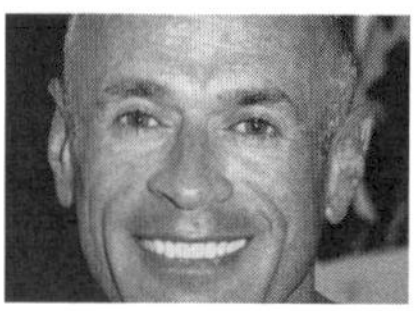

TIKO KERR, 1953
Meditations on Compassion; acrylic on canvas
2006; 36" x 48"

www.tikokerr. com

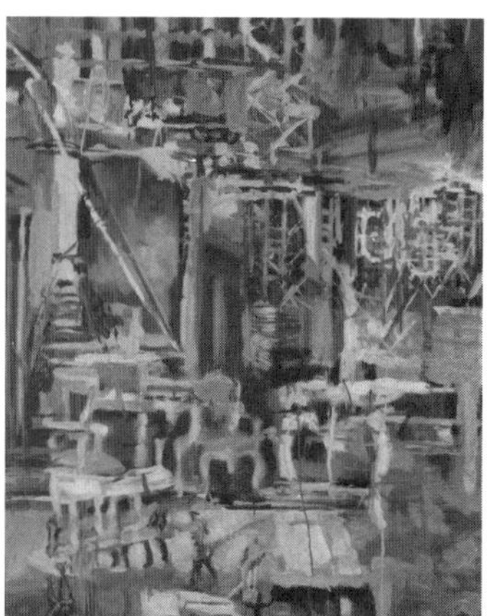

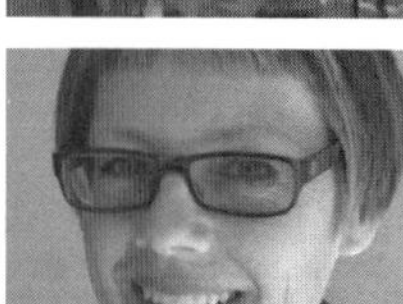

VAL NELSON, 1960
FGBG: oil on wood
2010; 60" x 48"

http://valnelson.ca

PROLOGUE

According to Hill Strategy Research Inc. (Canada), the three Canadian cities with the highest concentrations of artists are in British Columbia: They are Vancouver, Victoria and North Vancouver District Municipality. Their report, *Artists in Large Canadian Cities,* says that Vancouver has the highest concentration of artists among large Canadian cities (2.35%), a level that is three times the Canadian average (0.77%). Victoria has the second-highest concentration of artists (1.87%) and North Vancouver District Municipality has an artistic concentration of 1.61%. (The full report is available at www.hillstrategies.com.) For Canadian artists everywhere, there is a lot of competition; artistic density is not just an urban phenomenon.

In the face of all this competition, earning the interest of a commercial art gallery is a daunting task. Still, hundreds graduate from art school every year and other artists emerge without training to compete for the limited opportunities available in their local commercial galleries. From my experience, no issue interests contemporary visual artists more than gallery representation.

As an educator of visual artists, I have listened for over twenty years to the anticipated outcomes of commercial gallery representation from unrepresented artists. Here are my impressions of their expectations:

1) Emerging artists, artists who work in isolation, introverted artists and/or artists who are adverse to sales and self-promotion often expect the kind of relationship with their gallerist that they have had with a favoured parent, teacher or mentor. They expect guidance, direction and/or encouragement; often this is an unrealistic expectation.

2) They often think representation can yield unrealistic outcomes; they over-project their volume of sales and do not see representation as one aspect of a complex career.

3) They often do not realize the full cost of representation, including all preparatory costs such as documentation, transportation, framing, insurance, discounts, commissions, etc., as well as the marketing costs that are sometimes shared with the gallery.

4) They do not anticipate the kinds of unexpected issues that can arise with representation such as theft, non-payment, damage, returns, rejection, lack of sales, etc.

5) They often establish relationships with agents, organizations or galleries without doing due diligence; they can be too eager for exposure and income and suspend the critical judgment that is essential for a decision about representation.

To address the subject of representation, I invited four artists with considerable exhibition history in commercial art galleries to discuss their experiences. Kitty Blandy, Marcus Bowcott, Tiko Kerr and Val Nelson kindly agreed to talk with me. I met with them in Kitty's home. As a modest introduction to each of them, here are brief biographies they submitted.

1. **Kitty Blandy**

Kitty Blandy is a London-born, Vancouver-based artist who regularly exhibits internationally. Since her first solo show in London in 1986, Kitty has established a dedicated following, particularly in printmaking. Her working relationship with commercial galleries spans twenty-three years and includes more than ten galleries in London and Vancouver. Her work is included in many private and public collections, notably the National Portrait Gallery, London (bronze). Kitty works predominantly with printmaking, drawing and sculpture, on explorations of extreme physiognomic form and states of being. Recent work explores anthropomorphism and the human/animal hybrid.

2. **Marcus Bowcott**

Having lived for nearly 60 years by the sea, Marcus Bowcott's paintings often focus on the nuances and plentitude of the ocean. His paintings explore the often uneasy relationships between natural and industrial landscapes. His installations and sculptures explore human relations as well as our natural and altered environments. He completed his undergraduate studies in Vancouver and Toronto and received an MA from the Royal College of Art, School of Painting in 1984. Marcus has taught drawing and painting at Capilano University since 1991; he has exhibited regularly in private Vancouver galleries since 1986 as well as nationally and internationally. He is the recipient of several grants and awards, including grants from The Canada Council, The

Elizabeth Greenshields Foundation and The British Columbia Arts Council. His work is in several private and corporate collections and also in public collections, including The Canada Council Art Bank, Citizenship and Immigration Canada and The Vancouver Art Gallery.

3. **Tiko Kerr**

Sparked by a desire to record history, Tiko Kerr's art reveals his passion for life. There is nothing quiet about his work; every piece is loud and reflective of his state in life. He is adventurous with his subjects and has an ability to take the ordinary and present it in an extraordinary way. His work chronicles his own experiences and creates a visual archive of his life. At the core of each piece is a genuine truth that helps us discover and rediscover a moment in time.

4. **Val Nelson**

After completing the four-year Media Arts Program with Honours at Emily Carr College of Art + Design in 1988, Val Nelson received the Helen Pitt Award and was included in a group exhibition at the Vancouver Art Gallery. In ensuing years, she collaborated with dance artists, creating award-winning short videos that were screened across North America and Europe. In 1998 she began painting. Singled out by art critic Christopher Brayshaw for her work in *Artropolis 2003*, Val was a semi-finalist the same year in the Royal Bank Canadian Painting Competition. Val has received BC Arts Council and Vancouver Foundation grants, and she is included in *Carte Blanche Vol. 2: Painting*, a book on the current state of painting in Canada. Recently she was awarded an Artist's Grant to attend a Residency at the Vermont Studio Center.

INTERVIEW

Chris: Can you remember what outcomes you anticipated when you first sought representation?

Kitty: Well, to show and sell my work.

Chris: Did you expect to sell everything?

Kitty: I didn't think about that.

Chris: Did you expect to participate in marketing and promotion with your gallery, or did you expect the gallery to do all the work?

Kitty: When you're starting out, you don't think about those things. But yes, I did assume that the gallery would sell my work.

Chris: Did you hope to get critical reviews as well?

Kitty: Well, with the first galleries I was with, I knew there wouldn't be a critical element to it.

Chris: What did you expect in the way of exhibitions? How many would you expect to receive each year?

Kitty: I started when I was quite young. I didn't have any expectations at all.

Chris: Did you sign a contract?

Kitty: No.

Chris: Where was that?

Kitty: In London (UK).

Chris: What about you Val, do you remember your expectations when you started searching for a gallery?

Val: It wasn't that long ago actually and, like Kitty, I just wanted to show my work, communicate with an audience, and hopefully make some sales. I was just emerging; I shifted gears partway through a career in video, to intensively studying painting. I thought, "This is what I really want to do." But I didn't want to make it only for me, I wanted to communicate to an audience. I used to be a dancer; I like the idea of art communicating something. I like the idea of there being some kind of an exchange, so I thought the best of both worlds would be to create *and* to make a living. I didn't know if it would be possible, but I was willing to give it a go.

Chris: So obtaining representation was efficient and practical for you, given that you didn't have a mailing list.

Val: I didn't join an established gallery when I started out. Instead, I teamed up with a few other artists—very enterprising young women—who were running a little gallery. We were all trying to figure out how to make a career as artists; most of us were painters, collagists or photographers and I liked our energy together. When I talked to them, they said if I wanted to do a show, that I could pay a stipend for a month and that they'd help me hang and promote it.

Chris: And this was in Vancouver?

Val: Yes. And my show became something to work toward. It created a deadline, and I knew I had to make ten to twelve pieces for it. And out of that experience, I started to accumulate a mailing list by sitting in the gallery and meeting the people who came in. At first it was just friends, but then I started meeting complete strangers.

Kitty: So it was more like a cooperative gallery than a commercial gallery?

Val: It was not a commercial gallery at all, although we had the intention to help each other to attract an audience and hopefully make some sales.

Chris: Were all the people on your collective mailing lists invited to each person's individual exhibition?

Val: Yes, and we worked together to try and get media exposure. The great thing was that after getting my show up, I suddenly had this portfolio. Everything had all come together and I realized that I had all the tools with which to approach a commercial gallery.

Chris: Are you still working with that cooperative gallery ?

Val: No. It was only in business for about a year and a half, but after my show there, I had the portfolio, so I looked around at galleries in the community—just visiting, getting on the mailing list, seeing what they showed—and trying to see where I thought my work could fit in. The Bau-Xi Gallery had a good reputation for selling work, and they had a good range of artists, some of whom were a little more edgy, and I felt like my work would fit with them, so I made a submission and got in.

Young emerging artists, just starting to see where they fit, shouldn't send a submission to galleries without doing their homework. Does the gallery pay their artists? Do they offer solo shows? Talk to artists who are showing in the galleries that interest you and make sure that you know what you're getting into. Also, just going into the gallery and talking to staff can give you a sense of what it would mean to do business with them.. Bau-Xi has a very good reputation for always paying their artists, and representing their artists over a long period of time. With them, if your work changes, you know that they're not going to abandon you.

Chris: Do you remember what motivated you to first seek representation, Tiko?

Tiko: I was completely unschooled and self-taught. I'd been on the road for a number of years and had developed a kind of arrogance or cockiness about what I could do in the world. When I came back to Vancouver, I decided to get more serious about what I'd always done, which was to make art. I had never really taken it seriously before, so I started working really hard at painting and, once I'd accumulated a number of works, I just walked into Buschlen Mowatt Gallery and said, "I think you should show me." They were taken aback, but they agreed.

Chris: What did you think they would do for you?

Tiko: Sell my work and maybe give me some kind of professional validation, I guess.

Chris: What about you, Marcus, do you recall what you were seeking when you set out to find yourself a gallery?

Marcus: I lived in Langley and I started showing in local community shows as well as Young Contemporary shows in Vancouver. I also showed at a small gallery in White Rock that was owned and operated by a friend. In 1980, I went to London and returned in 1984 with an MA from the Royal College of Art, so I started teaching part-time at Emily Carr and taking my work around to galleries. Patrick Doheney, Director of the Heffel Gallery, liked my work and asked for a few pieces. He sold four or five of them within a day or so, and that bit of good luck helped get me my first solo show at the Heffel Gallery in 1988. Around that time, Ken Heffel passed away and his sons inherited the gallery; they transformed it into Heffel Fine Art Auction. Patrick left the gallery and I went with him to his new gallery, but the Patrick Doheny Gallery folded within a couple of years.

There was a period of time when I didn't have representation, so I represented myself in my studio at 1000 Parker Street. That was a wonderful time because of the Culture Crawl. I could charge less, and sold more. I mean, it's nice to have extra money to cover the bills in November and if you need to buy Christmas presents, right? And if somebody wanted a painting and could only afford a certain amount, I had the option of haggling and making a sale. It was a gas – and a lot of bloody work.

Now, I'm with Bau-Xi. I've been with them since '98 or '99. I had just finished with an exhibition at the Richmond Art Gallery, and it had been reviewed in Canadian Art and in local papers. I just walked in with some slides and documentation, like Tiko did.

Chris: Ross Penhall did the same thing at Buschlen Mowatt. He just walked in one day, but textbooks for artists say not to "cold-call" a gallery.

Tiko: You can't think about it too much or you'll scare yourself. It is a very intimidating experience to go in and show your work.

Kitty: I do think times have changed. There are more people who either are artists or think they're artists, and so to actually get someone to look at your work is very hard now, no matter how great your work may be. I think many proposals to galleries go unseen, unless you are introduced to the gallery by one of the gallery's artists. I still think cold calling is an unusual move; it's risky to approach a gallery in that way.

Val: Today, galleries might be off-put by that approach. As Tiko says, I think confidence is half the battle. I wanted to make sure I didn't step on any toes, so when I went into Bau-Xi, thinking about submitting my portfolio, I asked if they were taking submissions. The person I spoke to said they were, so I asked about their preferred presentation format and so forth, and what they would they like to see in the portfolio. And she said, "You're not doing still lifes are you? Because we already have enough artists working in that genre." So I explained that I was doing architectural work and she said, "OK, send us something." Then I left and mailed in a submission.

Chris: When you first got involved with your galleries, did it feel like entering into a partnership and that you'd be actively involved, or did you expect the gallery would do all the work?

Kitty: I've been involved in a number of galleries, and I would say there are no rules. With some, you're acting more as a partner, and with others, it's completely in their hands. Some have longer histories and are well established; others are newer and need all the help they can get. Depending on your relationship with the dealer, you can sometimes get involved. I've helped with hanging work at art fairs and with packing crates, but other times you just leave the work with the dealer and walk away.

Marcus: Selling out of Parker Street taught me a little of what it takes to run a gallery. You learn that you have to get in touch with people and develop a mailing list. You discover how to do the hard slog—when you sell something, you have to document it, contact people, deliver it or get it picked up, etcetera, and you realize what galleries do. Galleries have mailing lists, and those mailing lists are really valuable things because they've got a whole lot of art enthusiasts on them. I don't take my gallery for granted.

Chris: Do you get critical response to your work from your galleries?

Kitty: I don't think taking your work to a dealer, or showing your work in a commercial gallery, is going to yield a meaningful response to your work. You might have great support, you might sell your work, and you might meet a lot of people who connect with your work, but don't expect insight if you're showing in a commercial gallery. You do meet the odd dealer who is extremely engaged in their work—they all love art—but for them, it's a business. I don't see how you can validate your artistic expression from them.

Marcus: I agree with you. Commercial success isn't curatorial success or critical success, all of which are extrinsic.

Chris: Might not the dealer, on some occasions, secure a critical review?

Kitty: It depends on the gallery you're with.

Val: There are some writers who will visit commercial galleries for certain types of work. Marcus has had some critical writings about work he's shown in a commercial gallery.

Chris: Who makes that connection to the critic, the gallery or the artist?

Marcus: Well, for the most recent exhibition at the Evergreen Cultural Centre, I got in touch with Kevin Griffin at *The Sun*, and Bettina Matzkuhn, who wrote a review for *Canadian Art Online*. Bettina had previously written about my work, and Tiko's as well. I sent email images to other critics as well, but they didn't respond. All you can do is send out your images plus what you've written about your work, and hope they're moved. Just get word out to the critics, and if they pick it up, great; if they don't pick it up, you've done your best, and get on to the next project.

Val: I contacted Kevin as well. I did my own press release. I've been getting more involved in writing my own press materials in the last several years, and I think it's paying off. Gallery staff are very busy and you're not the only artist in their gallery. You can send them an artist's statement, but they don't have a lot of time to really absorb it, so you need to make sure that it's *your* message that the media receives.

Kitty: Galleries may be showing your work, but they're not your voice. That's why you need to be involved.

Val: When you get involved, you'll get more out of it. You haven't any control over what people think about your work, but as much as you can, you have to try and let people know what your work really means to you and help the gallery disseminate that information.

Chris: Is there an emotional impact when you successfully secure representation? Does it change your professional self-image?

Tiko: I think it really changed for me and I think it changed for other people. It seems to me that every second person in Vancouver is an artist, so when you can say that you have a show at a gallery, then people take you more seriously.

Kitty: You say it changes for others, but I think it does change for us too.

Val: It can help to build confidence and can feel like a validation when what you've been experimenting with in your studio is exhibited. Getting shown said to me, "Hey, maybe I'm on the right track. Maybe I should keep going with this!"

Chris: And you mentioned, Tiko, that exhibitions give you a deadline?

Tiko: Yes. I love having a deadline.

Chris: It gives you structure?

Tiko: It gives structure, and it also gives you focus.

Marcus: I love deadlines as well, but I also hate them because sometimes things end up dead at the line, so to speak.

Chris: Do you sometimes feel your gallery only wants work of a certain style?

Marcus: It's never really stated in that way, but yes. I'm really aware of the fact that I don't want to have to survive only on my art. I don't want to have to be dependent on it.

Tiko: I assume you mean that you don't want to have to rely solely on your work for your income; that you want to be able do the work that *you* want to do.

Kitty: Or, if your work is moving in a direction that the gallery's not going, that you can still survive if you have some teaching income or have some other way to earn income.

Marcus: Yes. That's it precisely. I've completed a painting and thought, "Well, this piece will sell!" only to discover that the galleries' and the public's taste doesn't match my own. Over time, you get a sense of what may sell and what doesn't, but I don't want to be tied to the yoke of having to sell a certain type of work. It's the antithesis of being your own artist.

Val: It can definitely be a trap; you have to be careful and make sure you're not compromising what you really want to say—what you really want to get at in your work.

Marcus: Yes, sometimes having to stick to a specific focus can help further development of the overall body of work. Sometimes you can be working on a series that requires development and you have to create another image that you didn't expect you'd have to do. Things transpire, and you find yourself pushing your ideas more.

Chris: Can't you do some work to make money and do another series focused on aesthetics? Is there something wrong with that?

Val: I would like to think that one can do what one really loves doing and find a market for it or, at least, find people who appreciate it whether they buy it or not.

Chris: Could you create market work using a pseudonym?

Val: You know, I thought I could. I had a strategy about five years ago that I would do just that, but the work was crap; it was terrible. They were bad paintings because I wasn't committed to them. They didn't come from the right place.

Kitty: There's no honesty in that. I think if you take your skills and do something completely different and not other paintings—that could work.

Chris: In an art survey of people who had bought art over a period of several years, the vast majority of them expressed a desire to know the artist. When you are represented by a gallery, how do consumers connect with you?

Kitty: They come to the opening. At an opening, people want to talk to you all night, and you have to put your happy face on. When they ask me what the work is about, I just say, "What do *you* think it's about?" I ask them, because they usually want to tell you what *they* think.

Tiko: I've always been under the impression that people buy work because they either like the work or they like, and/or know, the artist. When I am showing at a commercial gallery, I do an "artist talk" to the staff, so that they get a really good sense of what I'm trying to achieve. And that way, they can effectively represent me to their customers.

Chris: Given that several of you have referred to being with more than one gallery, what drives you to change galleries?

Kitty: When I was starting out, I was delighted that a gallery with a good reputation wanted to show my work—but then the gallerist retired and the gallery closed. Not a problem; that was fine. I moved on. But there have been at least three or four galleries that I've had to leave because of non-payment.

Chris: I'm amazed! Three or four!

Tiko: I've left two galleries for the same reason.

Chris: Were these unfortunate situations in spite of a contractual relationship with the dealer?

Kitty: I've only signed contracts for specifics shows such as art fairs and solo exhibition that specified details like delivery time, deadlines for mailing lists and cost share expectations etcetera. Only two of the ten galleries that have represented me had a general contract, and I had to take them both to court for non-payment. So that's why I say to go with your gut instinct when you are choosing a gallery.

Marcus: I suppose I've had a kind of contract, because the Bau-Xi has a price list that we both agree on for each show, and there have been times when I've said that some pieces aren't adequately priced, and we've revised them.

Tiko (to Marcus): So what is your arrangement when it comes to being paid? If there's no contract, is it understood that you're paid within thirty days?

Marcus: I get paid within the month, but if it's art rentals—and a couple of years ago, there weren't a lot of sales for me—rental payments would come through every three months or so.

Chris: Is the biggest problem with galleries about lack of payment?

Kitty: Well, I've also experienced questionable business practices (misrepresentation, for example) and galleries doing things with my work without telling me. I've submitted text for press releases to a gallery, only to see one of the staff just write their own text and circulate it.

Chris: They did that without your okay?

Kitty: They did it with no consultation whatsoever. Also, sometimes a gallery has put my work in places in which I didn't want it shown. That was a particularly bad experience. I've had a couple of galleries do that. Galleries sometimes seem to think that since they've got your work, they can do what they like with it.

Chris: Have you ever had work discounted?

Kitty: There's a standard 10% off for trade.

Chris: Five percent from the dealer and five from you?

Kitty: Yes, usually. But that's the other thing about your relationship with a dealer—you actually never know how much they sell your work for. You might get your sales receipt in the end, but you still don't *really* know its sale price unless you happen to know the collector who bought it.

Tiko: And that rarely happens. You rarely know where your work ends up.

Chris: Several of you have referred to mailing lists and their importance, but I often am told that galleries won't tell you who's bought your work. Shouldn't you be able to know who your customers are?

Val: Marcus and I are lucky. We get a statement at the end of every month that tells us the names of customers who buy our work. Getting the list demonstrates trust between the artist and the dealer. I have a dealer in Montreal who doesn't put the names on my statements, but I think they would if I asked.

Marcus: We get their names; we don't get all the contact information on the statements. If we want more information we simply ask.

Kitty: Although it is difficult, if you're an emerging artist and are eager to please, my advice is don't share your own mailing list! Often artists do; they walk in and share their lists. But I've known directors of galleries (mostly in the U.K.) who have been head-hunted, and they've been sought for the mailing list they have. I'm not saying people shouldn't use their mailing list, it's just that you should invite your list yourself, and not do so through the gallery. I'd suggest to artists to be very wary, because your list has value—especially if you have past buyers on it.

Val (to Marcus): Do you get emails directly asking if you do commissions, that kind of thing?

Marcus: No. Have you?

Val: Occasionally.

Chris: So if a stranger phoned you up and said, "Hey, I saw your show at Bau-Xi. Can I get your work directly from you?" What do you do?

Val: We have an arrangement with Bau-Xi for studio sales: The artist gets 60% and the gallery still gets 40%.

Marcus: I just had a show at the Evergreen Cultural Centre, and there were some pieces in it that Bau-Xi just didn't want to show. So I asked Bau-Xi, "What do we do here? Are you expecting a commission from this? What happens if I sell this?" And they said that I could sell that particular piece independent of them; that it was between Evergreen and me. Regardless, transactions need to be up front and transparent.

Chris: So you have an exclusivity arrangement with Bau-Xi in this particular market, but you can step outside that agreement with permission, and you negotiate that right each time. And your relationship with Bau-Xi isn't preventing you from being the artist you want to be. You're finding different venues for different forms of expression so that you're satisfied, and using Bau-Xi for one aspect of your work.

Marcus: That's right. My work is quite varied—all over the map really, in terms of mediums and approaches. I'm not interested in confining myself to what a gallery, or anyone else thinks as my "signature." I had a show at the grunt gallery in which I installed a live bull and projected cave paintings of wounded bison and labyrinths onto it. That's just not up Bau-Xi's alley. It would be nice if they were interested in exhibiting me as a "complete" artist—paintings, stacked car sculptures, bulls, warts and all—but that's not the way it is. Maybe they're saving me from myself. They've got their brand, or signature style, in which some of my paintings may fit. That's just the way it is, if I want to show my other work I seek out artist run centres and public galleries.

Tiko: Like Marcus, I was also with the Heffel Gallery and there was no exclusivity at all. They felt that the more my work was seen out in the community, the better for everybody. There were no constraints when it came to selling out of my studio, but I certainly would never sell with another gallery in the same market or anything like that. I left them only because the auctions were getting so successful that they didn't want to have shows anymore.

Kitty: They had the liberty of that policy because their main business was so predominantly in secondary sales. A lot of gallerists just can't give you that freedom.

Val: I have a gallery that might be seen as more commercial, so it's up to me to go to the public galleries or the alternative spaces and say, "Have a look at this." When I have work that's outside the mandate of my commercial gallery, I understand that I have to do the leg work. I don't want to limit myself; I want to be seen in a critical context as well as commercial. So it takes a little extra effort.

Marcus: It takes a *lot* of extra effort!

Val: You're right. And trying to keep up with your studio practice and the rest, it's a real juggling act.

Marcus: I feel that the art market in Vancouver is quite divergent. Some of the work seems to be all about the head, it's conceptual but the head is disconnected from the body. It doesn't have much sensuous engagement. On the flip side, there's a lot of work in commercial galleries that's more sensuous, and in some cases more spiritual, but unfortunately a lot of that work doesn't engage the brain. And so there is, in a certain sense, a lack of integration between body and mind. I'd like to see more work that's, at once, more critically and sensuously integrated.

Kitty: We don't have much written discourse here. We don't really have art critics; it's very difficult for writers about art to survive.

Chris: Critics have disappeared because the media that support them have disappeared. It is much more difficult to get media exposure for an artist nowadays, but the Internet has greatly enhanced direct sales opportunities. Do you think, in the future, that the role of the gallery is going to change?

Val: I think it's already changed for artists such as Thrush Holmes who just became his own "empire." I didn't think he even had a gallery, and the next thing you know, he's showing at Museum of Contemporary Canadian Art. He's just very good at self-promotion and he initially circumvented galleries. I think he was following the Damien Hirst model, saying, "Here I am," creating spectacle and doing it very well. And thank goodness! He's a fabulous painter. He's completely fearless. I think his experience is a different kind of model. We can't all be that outgoing though. He's comfortable with performing in public and self-promotion.

It does seem that the Internet is bringing some compensatory value to artists today, and it will likely be more important in the future as some of the traditional mediums for critical writing and curatorial response diminish.

Marcus: I just saw *The Mona Lisa Curse* by Robert Hughes. In it, he talks about the economic crash on Wall Street and the inflated art market as being related, and that there's madness in the art market. He thinks it sad that money, fame, and art have been so smashed together, and that people confuse fame with actual artistic expression. He says a lot of contemporary collection is by "second rate" collectors who are just going out and indulging in the big fashion of the day.

Chris: And how do you think that affects art buyers here at home?

Kitty: I don't think it does.

Val: We're not at that level. Which maybe is a good thing, because people here are, hopefully, buying work for the right reason. They buy things that they want to live with—I'm talking about private collectors who bring the artist's work into their home because they want something that makes them think about their world, or gives them an emotional response. I don't think that's going to go away.

Marcus: In some ways I feel like landscape painting is popular in Vancouver because most of our population is so new to this landscape; they want to somehow digest it through art, to somehow bring it into their homes and lives.

Kitty: I think we need to give people permission to like work that actually makes them feel good or that prompts them to ask themselves, "How did they do that?"

Marcus: One thing about Vancouver is that we are producing a lot of art school graduates who are producing a lot of art, and given there's only a very small market here, some are moving out into the bigger world and managing out there.

Chris: If a cohort of graduating fine art students were here, is there anything you would say to them about representation as they go out into the world?

Val: Learn how to write. Practice writing. And learn to be okay with speaking about your work. It starts with one little talk.

Chris: Val, what makes you emphasize learning writing skills?

Val: I found writing very difficult at first, because I'm a very visual person. However, I can spell and I know how to make a complete sentence, and that was a good start. I thought the work should speak for itself, but today, that is not enough.

Marcus: I've somehow managed to learn to write, albeit with a lot of kicking and screaming along the way. Becoming literate isn't just for the practical stuff either, it's necessary for developing ideas about your own personal work and how it relates to this life, this world. I recommend reading George Orwell's *Politics and the English Language* as a good place to start regarding visual art and the written word. When I started out, way back in the early seventies, I had the idea that written expression and visual art existed in separate worlds. I had learned to draw and paint, but felt uncomfortable with writing.

Kitty: I would advise students to be really confident, as you guys were when you walked into your first gallery, but not to be disdainful of galleries. Do not expect galleries to do everything for you, and realize that you may have to participate financially in your shows. And don't be afraid of putting a show together for yourself.

Putting your own show together is a good thing to do because you learn all the little details involved with exhibiting, so that when you are represented, you know why you're paying the 50% commission. The good galleries work hard for you. You shouldn't assume they're going to rip you off, but neither should you be naïve. Don't be a prima donna when you come out of school. You might have done very well and won an award at your grad show, but that doesn't mean you're going to be a superstar. You have to do the work.

Marcus: I think one of the big rewards of being an artist is just simply being an artist: Questioning what you see and engaging a way to manifest that sense of sight. You're probably naïve if you think that you're going to make a regular income at it. I heard this great quotation from an artist friend who had a day job as a copy writer: "You can make a killing with your art, but you can't make a living on it." I've had times when I've really done well, and it's almost unexpected. You do the "hard slog," and all of a sudden, you make some money out of the blue. But to expect that you're going to do so, month in and month out, well that's a big weight to put on your art. I think there's a lot to be said for having the freedom to express yourself through your medium and let that be.

Tiko: If you are going to be taking art seriously and making your living as an artist, you have to treat it as a business. You have to be conscious of taxes, for example. When I started out, I wasn't smart about my finances, so years later, Revenue Canada came after me. So get yourself an accountant, and keep receipts for everything!

Marcus: The administration that comes with being an artist is a lot of work and it takes away from your time in the studio, but you have to do it, you have to track all your write offs and expenses or the revenue man/woman will be staring at your book keeping.

Chris: Another lesson you mentioned is the value of the networking that you do. Being an artist is more than staying at home and painting in your studio.

Val: Be in your community; get involved. Engage with other artists to start with; we feed off each other, we generate energy, we keep each others' spirits up.

Tiko: This goes back to our conversation about having an outlet for how your work is perceived—I get my best feedback from other artists who are really, really honest.

Marcus: 1000 Parker Street was a fantastic place to be because it was somewhat akin to being in art school. Half the time, I found myself saying, "I can't talk right now, I've got to paint." But then, the next thing you know, you'd be having a coffee or a sandwich with some other artists and having a talk, challenging each other's ideas. It's important, that contact.

Tiko: I'd advise students to document their work from day one. Photograph it and write about it. It's much easier to do now that we have access to digital technology.

Kitty: If we're still talking about representation, students should know that it is the responsibility of the commercial galleries to keep proper inventory lists. The reputable galleries I've been with made it their job to make consignment lists and ensure that they were scrupulously correct. I was a printmaker, and it's very easy for an artist who makes multiples to just pop into the gallery and leave things without getting a consignment list, but you can't do that. There's no record of you leaving that work when you do that. Even if you make a list of the work you are dropping off on a scrap of paper and get someone from the gallery to sign it, you'll have a receipt for everything you leave. You should always arrive with your own list, but it's much better to have the gallery make two receipts for both of you to sign, and you keep one copy. It's not that they intentionally do not add your work to your inventory list, it's just that the gallery staff can get busy and can forget.

Chris: Every gallery represents many artists. It's important to remember that when we secure representation.

Kitty: It certainly is when you're choosing a gallery. If you have a choice, sometimes it's better to go with a gallery that doesn't have too many artists, because you'll get more service. But we don't always have that choice.

Marcus: I came across a book called *The $12 Million Stuffed Shark: The Curious Economics of Contemporary Art*, (by Don Thompson). He talks about there being 800,000 represented artists living in New York and London— approximately 400,000 in each city. He says that about 75 of them are "superstar" artists earning seven figures or more, annually. Below them, there are an astonishingly small number of artists—maybe 300—who are making six figures or more, annually. They are doing very well and don't have to teach or do other work in order to get by. Then there are about 5,000 artists he describes as having some sort of profile with gallery representation, but have to teach, or do some other type of work to fill the gap.

But don't stop doing your work because it's a valuable thing to do for intrinsic reasons; it's not just about extrinsic reward. I can't imagine my life not doing my art.

Tiko: It was really interesting to discover that on our $20 bill, we have a quotation that says, "Could we ever know each other in the slightest without the arts?" (Gabrielle Roy, 1909 – 1983) I think that's a very important and essential Canadian ideal for us to know and remember.

Another thing I wanted to say is that many artists have a hard time letting go of their best work. You really have to get over that. They sometimes like to hoard their best work, but I have come to the conclusion that we "give birth" to the things we create. They are our children and we must send them out into the world to have a life. Somehow, thinking that way really liberated me.

Val: I would add that for each body of work, try and keep one piece. It's a way to hold onto different aspects of your creative process through your lifetime, and it's going to be really interesting for you decades later. Also, frankly, it could be a nice little "pension" for you later on. You don't know, but at some point, a museum might come calling, or a prominent collector, and if your work has accrued in value over your career, you reap the rewards.

Tiko: Yes. I agree. I do series of prints and just archive them for something to rely on later on.

EPILOGUE

Representation is a partnership. It can be a wonderful and rewarding experience if, as in a marriage, both parties are in it for the long term, have mutual trust and are honest with each other. And like a marriage, the absence of these qualities can sour your relationship with your gallery.

Representation does not lessen your responsibilities, as many artists believe. In fact, representation can increase your administrative and creative workload. And, as the artists on this panel acknowledge, the art market and art marketing methodologies are changing. The Internet provides artists with the opportunity to invest the money they would otherwise pay as commission, in self-representation. I was happy to hear the panel of artists discuss the importance of a complex career; representation is only one aspect of their career. Artists must remember, one outcome of representation is the sudden and dramatic loss of half the income generated by your gallery sales.

Representation must, therefore, be part of a serious re-evaluation of your entire practice. You must consider carefully the impact of representation on your practice.

My students often envisage fame and fortune when I ask them about the impact of representation. Instead, I encourage a consideration of far more practical issues. How might representation affect your use of career time? How will the payment of commissions affect your practice and life? For answers to these and other questions, I refer my students to peers with experience. The insights that you may glean in this chapter and/or other chapters equate to those that can accrue to you through involvement with a community of artists. All my professional writing is proof of the value of peer assembly and the insights that it can provide.

Half of the artists in this panel are represented by Bau-Xi Gallery, a gallery that is very well known and respected. Consequently the conversation recorded in this chapter does not reflect my experience. Unfortunately, too many artists suffer adverse consequences as a function of representation. I say so, not to discourage you, but to reinforce Kitty's message not to be naïve. You cannot abrogate responsibilities when you engage the services of an agent or gallery; even in a trusting relationship, you are, and always will be, master of a complex career.

At the end of our session, the participating artists acknowledged the value of our time together. They enjoyed being in the company of peers and talking about professional issues. Salons are a concept with which artists are familiar—they were a form of peer assembly. We are used to critique sessions wherein peers share their response to our work, but it is not often that artists gather to discuss non-aesthetic professional development issues.

Don't be afraid to open your studio up one day, and invite some artists over to discuss your careers and/or practices. You can even work together on Facebook or email to establish an agenda that is compelling. Otherwise, joining an online artist collective, an arts council or a drawing group in your community can become your professional network, as can enrolling in the Continuing Studies program of your local college or university. Involvement with your peers can be as professionally rewarding as representation.

LINKS

Bau-Xi Gallery: www.bau-xi.com
Evergreen Cultural Centre: www.evergreenculturalcentre.ca
Hill Strategies Research Inc: www.hillstrategies.com
Museum of Contemporary Canadian Art: www.mocca.ca
Royal College of Art (London): www.rca.ac.uk
Thrush Holmes: www.thrushholmesempire.com

ABOUT THE AUTHOR

Chris Tyrell researches, teaches, writes and publishes about professional development for visual artists, seeking to maximize the pleasure, productivity and success of the creative practitioners he deeply respects and admires.

Chris has been involved with the visual arts, visual artists and the arts in general since 1976 when he established Presentation House Gallery of Photography in North Vancouver, BC. He designed, built and managed Presentation House Theatre and he has managed other performing arts venues. He was a founding member of the BC Touring Council and co-founded the Alliance for Arts and Culture in Vancouver.

Chris founded the *Visual Arts Newsletter* of Opus Framing & Arts Supplies in 1986. His editorials earned two *Vancouver Business and the Arts* awards.

Chris is currently an instructor of professional development at Emily Carr University of Art and Design in the Continuing Studies Department.

www.christyrell.ca

LINKS DIRECTORY

Alcuin Society: www.alcuinsociety.com
Alliance for Arts and Culture: www.allianceforarts.com
American Watercolor Society: www.americanwatercolorsociety.com
Architectural Institute of BC: www.aibc.ca
Art in Motion: www.artinmotion.com
Artists in Canada: artistsincanada.com/php/~studio.php
Artists in our Midst: http://www.artistsinourmidst.comArtStarts in the Schools: http://artstarts.com
Art Students' League: www.theartstudentsleague.org
Ballet British Columbia: www.balletbc.com
Banff Centre: www.banffcentre.ca
Bau-Xi Gallery: www.bau-xi.com
Buschlen Mowatt Gallery: www.buschlenmowatt.com
Caldwell Snyder Gallery: www.caldwellsnyder.com
Canada Council: www.canadacouncil.ca
Canadian Art Prints: www.canadianartprints.com
CARFAC Copyright Collective: www.carcc.ca
Cargoh: www.cargoh.com
Cheaper Show: http://thecheapershow.com
Circle Craft and their Christmas Market: http://www.circlecraft.net
Constant Contact http://search.constantcontact.com
eBay: www.ebay.ca
East Side Culture Crawl: www.eastsideculturecrawl.com
Elissa Cristall Gallery: www.cristallgallery.com
Etsy: www.etsy.com
Evergreen Cultural Centre: www.evergreenculturalcentre.ca
Facebook: www.facebook.com
Federation of Canadian Artists: http://artists.ca
Flickr: www.flickr.com
Gamblin Paints: www.gamblincolors.com
Granville Island Public Market: http://www.granvilleisland.com
Harvest: www.getharvest.com
ian tan gallery: www.iantangallery.com

Ílsensk Grafík: www.islenskgrafik.is
Island Sweet: www.islandsweet.etsy.com (Shawn O'Hagan)
Klondike Institute of Art and Culture: http://www.kiac.org
La Raza Group: www.larazagroup.com
Lian Zhen: www.lianspainting.com
Louis Vuitton: www.louisvuitton.com
Lucy Hogg: http://lucyhogg.com
Madrona Gallery: www.madronagallery.com
MailChimp http://www.mailchimp.com
Main Street Art Drift: www.thedrift.ca
Malaspina Printmakers: www.malaspinaprintmakers.com
Moss Street Paint In: http://aggv.ca/events/gallery-paint-in
Museum of Contemporary Canadian Art: www.mocca.ca
Nanaimo Art Gallery: www.nanaimogallery.ca
North East Watercolor Society: www.northeastws.com
Nes Artist Residency: http://neslist.is
New Leaf Editions: www.newleafeditions.com
Ocean Wilderness Inn: www.oceanwildernessinn.com
One of a Kind Show: www.oneofakindshow.com
Painter's Lodge: www.painterslodge.com
Palazzo Ricasoli: http://www.ricasoli.net (Florence)
PayPal: www.payPal.ca/ca
Preview Magazine: www.preview-art.com
Public Dreams Society: http://publicdreams.org
Res Artis: www.resartis.org
Royal College of Art (London): www.rca.ac.uk
Sakura: www.sakuraofamerica.com
Skype: www.skype.com
Sooke Fine Arts Show: /www.sookefinearts.com
Terence Robert Gallery: www.terencerobertgallery.com
Textile Museum of Canada: www.textilemuseum.ca/
Trans Artists: www.transartists.org
Thrush Holmes: www.thrushholmesempire.com
Tom Lynch: www.tomlynch.com
Twitter: http://twitter.com

Wendy D: http://wendyd.com (for Culture Crawl marketing workshops)
Vancouver Farmers' Markets: http://www.eatlocal.org
Windsor gallery: www.winsorgallery.com

For information about the **Parker Street** and **William Street Studios**, the **Artist Resource Centre** (ARC) and other artist studio collectives, please visit the **Eastside Culture Crawl** address and click on "Buildings."